BROOKLANDS
BOOKS

HIGH PERFORMANCE
MUSTANGS
1982-1988

Compiled by
R.M. Clarke

ISBN 1 870642 023

Distributed by
Brooklands Book Distribution Ltd.
'Holmerise', Seven Hills Road,
Cobham, Surrey, England
Printed in Hong Kong

BROOKLANDS BOOKS

BROOKLANDS BOOKS SERIES
AC Ace & Aceca 1953-1983
AC Cobra 1962-1969
Alfa Romeo Alfasud 1972-1984
Alfa Romeo Alfetta Coupes GT.GTV.GTV6 1974-1987
Alfa Romeo Guilias Berlinettas
Alfa Romeo Giulia Berlinas 1962-1976
Alfa Romeo Giulia Coupés 1963-1976
Alfa Romeo Spider 1966-1987
Allard Gold Portfolio 1937-1958
Aston Martin Gold Portfolio 1972-1985
Austin Seven 1922-1982
Austin A30 & A35 1951-1962
Austin Healey 100 1952-1959
Austin Healey 3000 1959-1967
Austin Healey 100 & 3000 Collection No. 1
Austin Healey 'Frogeye' Sprite Collection No. 1
Austin Healey Sprite 1958-1971
Avanti 1962-1983
BMW Six Cylinder Coupés 1969-1975
BMW 1600 Collection No. 1
BMW 2002 1968-1976
Bristol Cars Gold Portfolio 1946-1985
Buick Automobiles 1947-1960
Buick Riviera 1963-1978
Cadillac Automobiles 1949-1959
Cadillac Automobiles 1960-1969
Cadillac Eldorado 1967-1978
Camaro 1966-1970
Chevrolet Camaro & Z-28 1973-1981
High Performance Camaros 1982-1988
Chevrolet Camaro Collection No. 1
Chevrolet 1955-1957
Chevrolet Impala & SS 1958-1971
Chevelle & SS 1964-1972
Chevy II Nova & SS 1962-1973
Chrysler 300 1955-1970
Citroen Traction Avant 1934-1957
Citroen DS & ID 1955-1875
Citroen 2CV 1948-1988
Cobras & Replicas 1962-1983
Cortina 1600E & GT 1967-1970
Corvair 1959-1968
Daimler Dart & V-8 250 1959-1969
Datsun 240z 1970-1973
Datsun 280Z & ZX 1975-1983
De Tomaso Collection No. 1
Dodge Charger 1966-1974
Excalibur Collection No. 1
Ferrari Cars 1946-1956
Ferrari Cars 1962-1966
Ferrari Cars 1969-1973
Ferrari Dino 1965-1974
Ferrari Dino 308 1974-1979
Ferrari 308 & Mondial 1980-1984
Ferrari Collection No. 1
Fiat-Bertone X1/9 1973-1988
Fiat Pininfarina 124+2000 Spider 1968-1985
Ford Falcon 1960-1970
Ford Mustang 1964-1967
Ford Mustang 1967-1973
High Performance Mustangs 1982-1988
Ford RS Escort 1968-1980
Honda CRX 1983-1987
High Performance Escorts MkI 1968-1974
High Performance Escorts MkII 1975-1980
Hudson & Railton Cars 1936-1940
Jaguar XK120 XK140 XK150 Gold Portfolio 1948-1960
Jaguar Cars 1957-1961
Jaguar Cars 1961-1964
Jaguar MK2 1959-1969
Jaguar E-Type 1961-1966
Jaguar E-Type 1966-1971
Jaguar E-Type V12 1971-1975
Jaguar XKE Collection No. 1
Jaguar XJ6 1968-1972
Jaguar XJ6 Series II 1973-1979
Jaguar XJ6 & XJ12 Series III 1979-1985
Jaguar XJ12 1972-1980
Jaguar XJS Gold Portfolio 1975-1988
Jensen Cars 1946-1967
Jensen Cars 1967-1979
Jensen Interceptor Gold Portfolio 1966-1986
Lamborghini Cars 1964-1970
Lamborghini Cars 1970-1975
Lamborghini Countach Collection No. 1
Lamborghini Countach & Urraco 1974-1980
Lamborghini Countach & Jalpa 1980-1985
Lancia Stratos 1972-1985
Land Rover 1948-1973
Land Rover Series II & IIa 1958-1971
Land Rover Series III 1971-1985
Land Rover 90 & 110 1983-1989
Lotus Cortina 1963-1970
Lotur Elan Gold Portfolio 1962-1974
Lotus Elan Collection No. 2
Lotus Elite 1957-1964
Lotus Elite & Eclat 1974-1981
Lotus Turbo Esprit 1980-1986
Lotus Europa 1966-1975
Lotus Europa Collection No. 1
Lotus Seven 1957-1980
Lotus Seven Collection No. 1
Maserati 1965-1970
Maserati 1970-1975
Marcos Cars 1960-1988
Mazda RX-7 Collection No. 1
Mercedes 190 & 300SL 1954-1963
Mercedes 230/250/280SL 1963-1971
Mercedes 350/450SL & SLC 1971-1980
Mercedes Benz Cars 1949-1954
Mercedes Benz Cars 1954-1957
Mercedes Benz Cars 1957-1961
Mercedes Benz Competition Cars 1950-1957

Metropolitan 1954-1962
MG Cars 1929-1934
MG TC 1945-1949
MG TD 1949-1953
MG TF 1953-1955
MG Cars 1957-1959
MG Cars 1959-1962
MG Midget 1961-1980
MGA Collection No. 1
MGA Roadsters 1955-1962
MGB Roadsters 1962-1980
MGB GT 1965-1980
Mini Cooper 1961-1971
Morgan Cars 1960-1970
Morgan Cars 1969-1979
Morris Minor Collection No. 1
Old's Cutlass & 4-4-2 1964-1972
Oldsmobile Toronado 1966-1978
Opel GT 1968-1973
Packard Gold Portfolio 1946-1958
Pantera 1970-1973
Pantera & Mangusta 1969-1974
Plymouth Barracuda 1964-1974
Pontiac Fiero 1984-1988
Pontiac GTO 1964-1970
Pontiac Firebird 1967-1973
Pontiac Firebird and Trans-Am 1973-1981
High Performance Firebirds 1982-1988
Pontiac Tempest & GTO 1961-1965
Porsche Cars 1960-1964
Porsche Cars 1964-1968
Porsche Cars 1968-1972
Porsche Cars in the Sixties
Porsche Cars 1972-1975
Porsche 356 1952-1965
Porsche 911 Collection No. 1
Porsche 911 Collection No. 2
Porsche 911 1965-1969
Porsche 911 1970-1972
Porsche 911 1973-1977
Porsche 911 Carrera 1973-1977
Porsche 911 SC 1978-1983
Porsche 911 Turbo 1975-1984
Porsche 914 Gold Portfolio 1969-1988
Porsche 914 Collection No. 1
Porsche 924 1975-1981
Porsche 928 Collection No. 1
Porsche 944 1981-1985
Porsche Turbo Collection No. 1
Reliant Scimitar 1964-1986
Riley 1½ & 2½ Litre Gold Portfolio 1945-1955
Rolls Royce Silver Cloud 1955-1965
Rolls Royce Silver Shadow 1965-1980
Range Rover Gold Portfolio 1970-1988
Rover 3 & 3.5 Litre 1958-1973
Rover P4 1949-1959
Rover P4 1955-1964
Rover 2000 + 2200 1963-1977
Rover 3500 1968-1977
Rover 3500 & Vitesse 1976-1986
Saab Sonett Collection No. 1
Saab Turbo 1976-1983
Studebaker Hawks & Larks 1956-1963
Sunbeam Tiger And Alpine Gold Portfolio 1959-1967
Thunderbird 1955-1957
Thunderbird 1958-1963
Thunderbird 1964-1976
Toyota MR2 1984-1988
Triumph 2000-2.5-2500 1963-1977
Triumph Spitfire 1962-1980
Triumph Spitfire Collection No. 1
Triumph Stag 1970-1980
Triumph Stag Collection No. 1
Triumph TR2 & TR3 1952-1960
Triumph TR4.TR5.TR250 1961-1968
Triumph TR6 1969-1976
Triumph TR6 Collection No. 1
Triumph TR7 & TR8 1975-1982
Triumph GT6 1966-1974
Triumph Vitesse & Herald 1959-1971
TVR Gold Portfolio 1959-1988
Volkswagen Cars 1936-1956
VW Beetle 1956-1977
VW Beetle Collection No. 1
VW Golf GTi 1976-1986
VW Karmann Ghia 1955-1982
VW Scirocco 1974-1981
VW Bus-Camper-Van 1954-1967
VW Bus-Camper-Van 1968-1979
Volvo 1800 1960-1973
Volvo 120 Series 1956-1970

BROOKLANDS MUSCLE CARS SERIES
American Motors Muscle Cars 1966-1970
Buick Muscle Cars 1965-1970
Camaro Muscle Cars 1966-1972
Capri Muscle Cars 1969-1983
Chevrolet Muscle Cars 1966-1972
Dodge Muscle Cars 1967-1970
Mercury Muscle Cars 1966-1971
Mini Muscle Cars 1961-1979
Mopar Muscle Cars 1964-1967
Mopar Muscle Cars 1968-1971
Mustang Muscle Cars 1967-1971
Shelby Mustang Muscle Cars 1965-1970
Oldsmobile Muscle Cars 1964-1970
Plymouth Muscle Cars 1966-1971
Pontiac Muscle Cars 1966-1972
Muscle Cars Compared 1966-1971
Muscle Cars Compared Book 2 1965-1971

BROOKLANDS ROAD & TRACK SERIES
Road & Track on Alfa Romeo 1949-1963
Road & Track on Alfa Romeo 1964-1970
Road & Track on Alfa Romeo 1971-1976

Road & Track on Alfa Romeo 1977-1984
Road & Track on Aston Martin 1962-1984
Road & Track on Auburn Cord & Duesenberg 1952-1984
Road & Track on Audi 1952-1980
Road & Track on Audi 1980-1986
Road & Track on Austin Healey 1953-1970
Road & Track on BMW Cars 1966-1974
Road & Track on BMW Cars 1975-1978
Road & Track on BMW Cars 1979-1983
Road & Track on Cobra, Shelby &
  Ford GT40 1962-1983
Road & Track on Corvette 1953-1967
Road & Track on Corvette 1968-1982
Road & Track on Corvette 1982-1986
Road & Track on Datsun Z 1970-1983
Road & Track on Ferrari 1950-1968
Road & Track on Ferrari 1968-1974
Road & Track on Ferrari 1975-1981
Road & Track on Ferrari 1981-1984
Road & Track on Fiat Sports Cars 1968-1987
Road & Track on Jaguar 1950-1960
Road & Track on Jaguar 1961-1968
Road & Track on Jaguar 1968-1974
Road & Track on Jaguar 1974-1982
Road & Track on Jaguar 1983-1989
Road & Track on Lamborghini 1964-1985
Road & Track on Lotus 1972-1981
Road & Track on Maserati 1952-1974
Road & Track on Maserati 1975-1983
Road & Track on Mazda RX7 1978-1986
Road & Track on Mercedes 1952-1962
Road & Track on Mercedes 1963-1970
Road & Track on Mercedes 1971-1979
Road & Track on Mercedes 1980-1987
Road & Track on MG Sports Cars 1949-1961
Road & Track on MG Sports Cars 1962-1980
Road & Track on Mustang 1964-1977
Road & Track on Peugeot 1955-1986
Road & Track on Pontiac 1960-1983
Road & Track on Porsche 1951-1967
Road & Track on Porsche 1968-1971
Road & Track on Porsche 1972-1975
Road & Track on Porsche 1975-1978
Road & Track on Porsche 1979-1982
Road & Track on Porsche 1982-1985
Road & Track on Rolls Royce & Bentley 1950-1965
Road & Track on Rolls Royce & Bentley 1966-1984
Road & Track on Saab 1955-1985
Road & Track on Toyota Sports & G T Cars 1966-1986
Road & Track on Triumph Sports Cars 1953-1967
Road & Track on Triumph Sports Cars 1967-1974
Road & Track on Triumph Sports Cars 1974-1982
Road & Track on Volkswagen 1951-1968
Road & Track on Volkswagen 1968-1978
Road & Track on Volkswagen 1978-1985
Road & Track on Volvo 1957-1974
Road & Track on Volvo 1975-1985
Road & Track Henry Manney At Large & Abroad

BROOKLANDS CAR AND DRIVER SERIES
Car and Driver on BMW 1955-1977
Car and Driver on BMW 1977-1985
Car and Driver on Cobra, Shelby & Ford GT40
  1963-1984
Car and Driver on Datsun Z 1600 & 2000
  1966-1984
Car and Driver on Corvette 1956-1967
Car and Driver on Corvette 1968-1977
Car and Driver on Corvette 1978-1982
Car and Driver on Corvette 1983-1988
Car and Driver on Ferrari 1955-1962
Car and Driver on Ferrari 1963-1975
Car and Driver on Ferrari 1976-1983
Car and Driver on Mopar 1956-1967
Car and Driver on Mopar 1968-1975
Car and Driver on Mustang 1964-1972
Car and Driver on Pontiac 1961-1975
Car and Driver on Porsche 1955-1962
Car and Driver on Porsche 1963-1970
Car and Driver on Porsche 1970-1976
Car and Driver on Porsche 1977-1981
Car and Driver on Porsche 1982-1986
Car and Driver on Saab 1956-1985
Car and Driver on Volvo 1955-1986

BROOKLANDS MOTOR & THOROUGHBRED & CLASSIC CAR SERIES
Motor & T & CC on Ferrari 1966-1976
Motor & T & CC on Ferrari 1976-1984
Motor & T & CC on Lotus 1979-1983
Motor & T & CC on Morris Minor 1948-1983

BROOKLANDS PRACTICAL CLASSICS SERIES
Practical Classics on Austin A 40 Restoration
Practical Classics on Land Rover Restoration
Practical Classics on Metalworking in Restoration
Practical Classics on Midget/Sprite Restoration
Practical Classics on Mini Cooper Restoration
Practical Classics on MGB Restoration
Practical Classics on Morris Minor Restoration
Practical Classics on Triumph Herald/Vitesse
Practical Classics on Triumph Spitfire Restoration
Practical Classics on VW Beetle Restoration
Practical Classics on 1930S Car Restoration

BROOKLANDS MILITARY VEHICLES SERIES
Allied Military Vehicles Collection No. 1
Allied Military Vehicles Collection No. 2
Dodge Military Vehicles Collection No. 1
Military Jeeps 1941-1945
Off Road Jeeps 1944-1971
V W Kubelwagen 1940-1975

CONTENTS

BROOKLANDS
BOOKS

ACKNOWLEDGEMENTS

Brooklands Books have grown out of a hobby that started over thirty years ago, and have today become one of the most accessable works of reference for those that enjoy automobiles.

Some 10,000 stories can be located within their 300 titles. They cover in the main affordable post-war vehicles that can be bought, restored and cherished by ordinary people.

The fastest selling titles within our series have been those that cover the muscle cars of the late sixties and early seventies, the Camaros Mustangs and Firebirds to name but three.

Part of our function is to recognise the cars in production today that will become the collectibles of tomorrow. We believe that the current Camaros Mustangs and Firebirds are such cars and we hope that by keeping stories written about them in print will encourage their owners to lovingly maintain them for the enthusiasts that will restore, drive and exhibit them at the turn of the century.

The leading automotive publishers have for many years generously supported our series by allowing us to include their copyright road tests and other articles that make up these anthologies. I am sure that Mustang devotees will wish to join with us in thanking the management of Autocar, Automobile, Car and Criver, Car Craft, Hot Rod, Motor, Motor Trend, Mustang, Road & Track, R&T Specials, and Sports Car World, for their understanding and ongoing help.

R.M. Clarke

0-60 in 6.9 secs. 302 GT Mustang

by Jim McCraw

You can feel it in the air and see it in the quickened pace of everyday business. Suddenly, the excitement, the energy, the pride are palpable. Even in the midst of severe economic problems, and after an absence of more than a decade, Ford Motor Company has decided to put itself back into racing and back into the high-performance production car business. It's a part of Ford's new marketing strategy. Public reaction to this return to big-league racing has been overwhelmingly positive; a whirlwind of mail has told the company to start building something that's quick, fast and fun to drive, like the Miller Zakspeed Mustang. Ford has responded with a high-performance 5-liter (302cid) HO engine package, applicable to all 1982 Mustang and Capri models, but best blended with the new Mustang GT or Capri RS.

The package was given the nod from the highest echelon of management and originally designated as a 1982½ addition. But the swell of enthusiasm at the marketing and engineering levels, and the speed with which engineering problems were solved, have pushed the program up to an Oct. 1 startup, only a couple of weeks after introduction of the 1982 Ford line.

The 302 V-8 was taken out of the Mustang lineup after 1979 and replaced by a smaller, weak-kneed 255cid V-8 sold only with automatic transmission and cruising gear ratios. A woefully inadequate turbocharged 4-cylinder combination was marketed but ultimately scrapped. The Mustang was losing image after 15 years on the market, in spite of a new body and a superior TRX handling package. Enter a new regime, a new commitment to competition and, in the early spring of this year, a program to wake up the 302 and the chassis it goes into, to build a new image leader.

Suddenly, the Mustang finds itself on a quicker track

The engine isn't all that radically changed, but it's almost 30 horsepower stronger, with nearly 6% more peak torque and a much higher, wider torque curve overall. The camshaft profile for the 302 HO engine was taken directly from the company's marine parts bin for more lift, duration and overlap time. Intake and exhaust valve diameters have not been changed, but exhaust valves for the HO engine are now nickel/chrome with flash-chromed stems. The nylon valve stem oil seals are larger and deeper for better high-rpm oil control. High-rpm valvetrain stability was assured with the substitution of a double-row roller timing chain for the standard link silent chain used in the regular 302 engine. Valve spring pressures were increased only slightly to cope with the higher rpm operation (the old 302 fell on its face over 4,000 rpm; the 302HO will be redlined at 6,000 rpm). The rest of the engine internals are standard 302, but a much-improved intake/carburetion/exhaust tract was incorporated.

For openers, the 302 HO uses an aluminum intake manifold with controlled heat to the carburetor, heat that is diverted once manifold temperature gets up to 90° F. The 310cfm 2-barrel carburetor from the '79 version was superseded for the HO package by a 356cfm Ford-built 2150A carburetor using 1.56-inch throttle

bores and a raft of "hot fuel handling" modifications. The "big" carburetor uses a 19% larger inlet needle and seat assembly, and a higher fuel level in the fuel bowl with an anti-slosh fix built into the gasket (for continuous fuel delivery even in severe cornering maneuvers). The mechanical fuel pump pressure has been upped from 6.5 to 8.5 psi, and the fuel system incorporates a return line that continuously reroutes some hot fuel back to the tank, where it cools down and returns to the fuel bowl. The air side of the air/fuel mixture is handled by a huge dual-snorkel air cleaner box with flexible rubber "zip tubes" connected to fender panels to draw cool air from behind each front tire. The air box/filter assembly is

derived from the 351cid LTD HO police engine package and is so huge that it requires the use of nonfunctional hood scoops for adequate clearance. On the exhaust side, straight-line 4-into-1 cast iron exhaust manifolds and twin 2¼-inch headpipes with a light-off catalyst empty into the main converter. From there, the system is 2½-inch pipe going through a single resonator and a twin outlet tip; there is no muffler, and very little backpressure in the system, even though it will pass the federal noise test easily.

Jim Clarke, the engineer in charge of 302 HO development, pointed out that the engine's ratings of 160 horsepower and almost 250 pounds-feet of torque are deceptive and that the engine installed

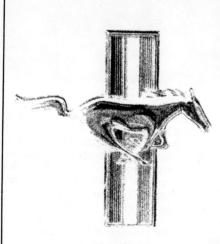

Homologation to homogenization and back: a history of the Mustang

by Robert Diefendorf

Back in the 2% inflation days of the middle Sixties, when drag coefficient was just an obscure physics term and nobody knew or cared about EGR and NOX, Ford Motor Company singlehandedly started a revolution by introducing a lightweight, nimble, inexpensive car that could melt pavement with a stab of the right foot. The first Mustang.

Return with us now to those thrilling days of yesteryear, and remember . . .

1964½: The Mustang was shoved in front of the public with a huge media campaign. It worked: 22,000 were ordered over the introductory weekend. But, for the performance-oriented buyer, patience was in order. The 260cid V-8 was good for only 160 horsepower.

1965: The fastback was added, and with it the 289 V-8. In its hottest form, with mechanical lifters, 10.5:1 compression ratio and 4-barrel carb, it produced 271 horsepower and 312 pounds-feet of torque. The 271-horsepower engine required the "special handling package"—higher-rate springs, heavy-duty shocks, larger front sway bar and quicker steering. *Sports Car Graphic* tested a 4-speed with 4.11 rear and recorded times of 7.5 seconds to 60 mph and 15.7 seconds for the quarter-mile. Not bad for a 3,290-pound car. It cost $3,854. But the Mustang was no competition for the high-horsepower 'Vettes or the GTO. Enter Carroll Shelby. Shelby-American dealers sold the GT 350 with 306 horsepower which was, in fact, a road-going race car—ultra-stiff suspension, fiberglass hood, side exhaust—and could reach 60 mph in about 6 seconds.

The light and nimble 1964½ Mustang

1966: Rent-a-Shelby. Incredibly, Hertz wanted a performance image, and for $25 a day and 25¢ a mile, you could rent a GT 350 with automatic and play SCCA racer for a day. The 271-horsepower 289 with "competition suspension package" continued to be the strongest engine/suspension offered by Ford.

1967: The 390cid big-block was introduced in the restyled Mustang, which had to be widened and stretched to accept the larger engine. In "Thunderbird Special" tune with 10.5:1 pistons, hydraulic lifters, mild cam and premium gas in the Holley 4-barrel, the 390 delivered 320 horsepower. (The 271-horsepower 289 was still available but cost twice as much as the 390.) With standard 3.90 rearend, the quarter-mile took 15 seconds. A special competition handling option with extra-stiff front and rear springs, extra-thick front sway bar, adjustable shocks, 16:1 *manual*

and running in a moving car is getting significantly more power to the ground under wide-open throttle than would normally be expected. This is because it has been fitted with a number of parasitic-loss fixes. At full throttle, the air conditioning compressor is cut out completely by a clutch on the drive hub; the Thermactor air pump is cut out completely, and the engine cooling fan is disengaged through a clutch mechanism on its hub, leaving the engine free to propel the car with minimum intake restriction and exhaust system backpressure to interfere with power production.

The 302 HO engine will be the first to appear according to Ford's new dress code. It will not be painted in all-over

Ford blue, but rather will be installed in natural iron and aluminum colors with ribbed cast aluminum rocker covers, black air cleaner/snorkel/zip tube assembly, grey 8mm spark plug wires, and a gray distributor cap (the 302 HO will use a Duraspark II ignition with magnetic trigger, 12° initial advance and 40° total advance at 4,000 rpm, with Motorcraft AFS42 spark plugs, one range colder than normal, and a 32 kV coil). One by one, all of Ford's engines will be converted to this appearance, influenced by European and Japanese practice.

The 302 HO will be sold as a package on any 1982 Capri or Mustang, including Ford's single-rail overdrive (SROD) 4-speed manual transmission, 3.08:1

Traction-Lok rear axle, power steering, power disc/drum brakes and handling suspension as mandatory add-ons with the engine. All 302 HO cars will get an additional suspension item, a gussetted, welded-on bar that attaches to the axle housing on each side. On acceleration, the axle housing rotates until the rubber-covered bar comes in contact with the lower control arm, effectively controlling wheelhop.

The car we tested was an extreme example of a top-of-the-line Mustang, now called the GT (Mustang models will be juggled for 1982 to parallel the Escort line: L, GL, GLX, and GT replacing the old Cobra line). The GT comes only as a 3-door hatchback, with P185/75R14 blackwall steel radial tires, handling suspension, fog lamps, black twin remote mirrors, cast aluminum wheels, console with graphic display, swivel map light, 4-spoke steering wheel and restricted colors. The GT will be offered only in red, black or metallic silver exteriors with red or black interiors, and there is a large amount of blackout trimming, including the entire dash and all knobs and controls, all exterior moldings, trim, door handles, mirrors and antenna. What remains will be body color, including the new nose, grille, spoilers front and rear, headlamp doors, cowl and lower back panel appliqué, for that lean and hungry

---

steering and wider rims and tires improved the 390's handling. But the big-block posed a weight distribution problem, which would plague all big-block Mustangs. Physically, the '67 Mustang was larger: front track increased 2 inches, length increased 2 inches overall, and the base weight—with 6-cylinder engine—was up 140 pounds.

1968: Very minor cosmetic changes were made, as compared to the major restyle of the previous year. This was the last year for the expensive 271-horsepower 289, and its replacement, the 302, was introduced. The big news—literally—was the availability of the 427, the 428 Cobra Jet and the Cobra Jet Ram Air 428.

The 427, with its five cross-bolted main bearings, 10.9:1 compression ratio and hydraulic cam, added up to 390 horsepower at 5,200 rpm and 460 pounds-feet of torque at 3,200 rpm. The Cobra Jet Ram Air 428 came with a functional, vacuum-actuated hood scoop, large ports and valves and a 735cfm Holley. Ford rated the engine at 335 horsepower with 440 pounds-feet of torque. The Shelby GT 500 was tested by *MT:* 0-60 mph in 6.5 seconds and a 14.75 quarter-mile.

Shelby production peaked, and construction of the cars was moved to Michigan. The GT 350 got the 302.

1969: Ford introduced the Mach I, the Boss 302—perhaps the best overall performance Mustang—and the mighty Boss 429. Both the Boss 302 and 429 were built for homologation purposes, the 302 for Trans-Am, the 429 for NASCAR.

Rated at 375 horsepower at 5,200 rpm with 450 pounds-feet of torque at 3,400 rpm, the

Boss 429 was awesome. The aluminum heads were O-ringed to the block; it had an aluminum intake manifold, forged connecting rods, forged steel crankshaft, pop-up pistons, 4-bolt main bearings, 750cfm Holley, solid lifters and a ram-air shaker hood scoop that was opened manually from the dashboard.

The suspension was heavy-duty, as could be expected. A heavy-duty 4-speed manual backed up the engine and transmitted the power to a 3.91 Traction-Lok rear.

More than 850 of the thinly disguised racing engines were produced for the 1969 model year, and 505 for 1970. The car cost more than $5,000 and wasn't much quicker than the Mach I with its Cobra Jet Ram Air 428.

The Boss 302 competed with the Chevy Z/28 in the Trans-Am series. The 302 engine was the heart of the car: 290 horsepower and 290 pounds-feet of torque. An aluminum high-rise manifold held a huge 780cfm Holley that gushed fuel through the canted-valve heads. The carefully engineered small-block had a forged steel crank, windage tray, 4-bolt main bearing caps on the three center bearings, forged rods, and aluminum pop-up pistons. It would rev to 7,000 rpm. A 4-speed with 3.50 rear was standard, with numerically higher rears available, up to a 4.30 in locker form, a setup that would do 0-60 in 5.5 seconds. Weight distribution was great, and with 16:1 steering and ventilated front discs, it was a road-going race car. It cost $3,720.

1970: Both of the Boss cars were continued, and the 351 Cleveland engine arrived. The Cleveland differed from Ford's Windsor in that the new engine had different heads with canted valves, and the block had an in-

Carroll Shelby's GT 350 and 427 Cobra

tegral water crossover passage to remove passages from the intake manifold. With super-high-compression 11.4:1 pistons, it produced 300 horsepower at 5,400 rpm. (This engine also found its way into the Pantera.)

The 428s were on their way out. However, for 1970, Ford added the 429 Super Cobra Jet, a smaller high-performance version of the 460cid Lincoln engine.

1971: A major redesign year, with the Mustang gaining weight and length. The Boss 302 was dropped and replaced by a 351 HO 4-barrel prepared by Holman and Moody. A trio of 429s were available for the Mach I. The 351 HO had a conservative rating of 330

look. Our red test car had additional options, including TRX suspension and tires, Recaro bucket seats, AM/FM cassette unit with premium sound system, air conditioning, rear defroster and the light group.

We spent the better part of three days driving, photographing, thrashing and generally investigating the GT 302 HO on Ford's Dearborn test track and on the streets nearby. Our opinion is that it's the best-balanced Mustang ever. It exhibits a combination of awesome acceleration, consistently short and powerful stopping, and flat, cat-quick handling.

The afternoon of one day went entirely for acceleration testing, where we went through nearly 50 full-throttle runs to measure acceleration in 10-mph increments from 0-30 through 0-100 mph plus quarter-miles, virtually nonstop. Throughout the day, there was no sign of weakness, oil loss, coolant loss, overheating or fuel percolation, even in Detroit's hot, humid weather. This indicates that, if nothing else, the 302 HO has guts by the bucketful. It took a number of runs to get the essential rhythm of clutch, gas and shifter down pat and produce consistent times. We found out early that Michelin TRX tires are terrific for handling but hardly ideal for dragstrip work. We had to leave the line at idle, get the car moving, and apply full throttle instantly to

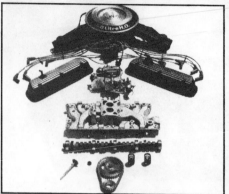

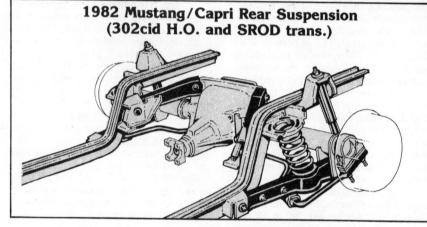

1982 Mustang/Capri Rear Suspension (302cid H.O. and SROD trans.)

The 1969 Boss 302.

horsepower with 4-bolt mains, forged and shotpeened rods, forged aluminum pistons, solid lifters and a hardened camshaft.

The strongest 429 Cobra Jet offered in '71 was the Super Cobra Jet. The 7- to 9-mpg engine was an improvement on the standard CJ and pumped its 375 horsepower and 440 pounds-feet of torque through a Detroit Locker rear encasing a 4.11 gear.

The front suspension geometry was revised, and the competition suspension system was again available.

1972: The big-inch engines and Boss models went away. Halfway through the model year, the performance hole was filled by a 351 4-barrel—dubbed the 351 Cobra Jet. The 275-horsepower engine could push the Mustang to 60 mph in 6.6 seconds.

1973: Performance wasn't part of the Mustang's vocabulary in '73. The price of a gallon of imported crude was on the rise, and

the public was looking favorably at the imported-car market.

1974: The Mustang II, Ford's response to changing times, was named Car of the Year. The Mach I, in fastback body only, came with the 2.8-liter German V-6, and we said it "combines a performance car with the utility of a hatchback and the economy of the Mustang II." However, even the Rallye Package—adjustable shocks, radial tires, limited-slip rear and stiffer springs and stabilizer bars—couldn't make up for the 0-60 time of 14.2 seconds.

1975: Deliverance from boredom came in the form of the 302 V-8. Hindered by an automatic transmission—the only transmission to be had—and a 3.00:1 rear, the V-8-equipped Mustang hustled to 60 mph in 9.6 seconds.

1976: Ah, yes, the Bicentennial, and to celebrate, the Mustang begat Son of Mustang: Cobra II. Resplendent in white with blue stripes or gold on black, front spoiler and rear lip spoiler, it was a Cobra in name only; the base engine was the anemic 2.3-liter four. The 302 V-8 was optional. The only saving grace was the fact that a 4-speed could be had behind the 302.

1977: Minor detail changes were made; the 302 V-8 continued to be the best Mustang offered.

1978: If flares, spoilers, phony hood scoops and loud paint helped to sell the Cobra II, why, thought Ford, we'll add some more and sell more cars! Enter the King Cobra, nothing more than a decal-and-paint variation on the Cobra II.

1979: The third major redesign of the Mustang. The key phrase for performance was TRX, as in TRX tires and suspension system. Equipped with the 302 V-8, 4-speed and Michelin TRX tires on aluminum wheels, it was a hit at *MT:* "We expected this combination to produce superior handling, but what we didn't expect was the total absence of increased noise, vibration and harshness that is usually part and parcel of such 'handling' kits." We also liked the 8.7-second 0-60 time.

The 2.3-liter, 132-horsepower turbocharged 4-cylinder engine—slightly slower than the 302 V-8—turned out to be less successful. Customers complained about its balkiness, and the Garrett AiResearch turbos started leaking oil. Production of the turbo engine was halted until the problems could be worked out. At the end of the year, the 2.8-liter German V-6 was replaced by the 3.3-liter (200cid) inline six.

To be as American as possible in sportiness and to reinforce a competitive image, the '79 Mustang was selected to be the Indy pace car. Pace car replicas—11,000 in all—found their way into Ford showrooms with Recaro seats and special paint and decal treatment.

1980-81: The 302 V-8 was replaced by a 255 V-8, with automatic only. The nose of the Indy pace car was grafted to the Cobra, and the Recaro seats were also carried over. Then, during the spring of this year, the 302 V-8 was revived, modified and readied for installation in 160-horsepower form, into all '82 Mustangs with a wide-ratio 4-speed overdrive manual and 3.08 gears. Once again, the Mustang's 0-60 capability is under 7 seconds.

The '82 Mustang GT will come only in red, black or silver, with red or black interior only, using blackout trim and body color with a minimum of chrome. The package includes handling suspension, P185/75R14 tires, cast aluminum wheels, fog lamps, dual remote mirrors, 4-spoke steering wheel, console, map light, a specific flat black dash trim, GLX seats and GL door panels. TRX suspension and Recaro seats are separate options, and all three optional engines can be had in GT Mustangs.

avoid turning the already whipped tires into smoking rubble. But once we got the rhythm down, the numbers came down accordingly to a best 0-60 performance of 6.9 seconds, 0-70 in 10.3 seconds, 0-100 in 21.1 seconds—the quickest times we've seen from a domestic car in many years. Yes, it was a prototype; yes, it did have the equivalent of 10,000 miles on the drivetrain (though the tires were brand-new); and yes, we were more than a little concerned that production versions would not, could not be as fast, but we were still impressed. Ford engineers assured us that production versions would be very close to prototype performance.

The nose-heavy Mustang (58% front/42% rear distribution) performed equally well on the brake test pad. With cold TRX tires and power disc/drum brakes, the car stopped straight and short: 30-0 in 40-41 feet, 60-0 in 159-161 feet, distances worthy of an all-disc Ferrari 308.

On Ford's own handling course at Dearborn, a well-paved, crowned course with a variety of rights and lefts and turn radii varying from 50 to 200 feet, a long final sweeper to the right and a sharp corner onto the "front straightaway," the GT with a horsepower injection was a revelation. Good enough to be the all-time course lap recordholder in the capable hands of chief vehicle development engineer Dan Rivard, several ticks slower in our own hands. With variable-ratio power assist for its rack-and-pinion steering, TRX suspension, wheels and tires, and plenty of usable torque passed through a

wide-ratio overdrive gearbox, the Mustang GT felt nearly invincible; much flatter, lighter and quicker than any Ford product we've taken around the course in 15 years of testing production cars at Dearborn. The stout brakes and relatively slick shifter allowed for easy heel-and-toe maneuvers, with eyes-on-the-road downshifting.

After more than 50 thoroughly hedonistic laps around the smooth-pavement handling course, we swung the GT around to the low-speed track. This circuit duplicates some of the worst paving and road surfaces in America in order to unmask noise, vibration and harness devils—which *had* to be hiding somewhere in these high-performance underpinnings. We simply gave up after four bone-jarring laps; driving with two wheels on flat surface and two on London blitz rubble didn't generate enough thump and shudder to complain about. After three years of experience with the Mustang, the engineers have managed to dial out all but a few noises and harshness sources. This GT is one buttoned-up automobile.

Ford's marketing plans are equally buttoned-up. From the beginning, there were parallel programs destined to come together as product. The GT package, as a replacement for the unsubtle, underwhelming Cobras of 1980-81, was to be understated and European in its appeal for the oft-cited "new buyer." The 302 HO engine was designed for across-the-board Mustang installation as a relatively low-priced appeal to repressed grass-

roots performance guys who are fed up with high prices and low performance. A 302 HO Mustang with a solid array of typical options in mid-level GL trim should be buyable at a price well under $10,000. A duplicate of our test car should be attainable for slightly under $12,000, right where the parallel programs meet at the top of the line. The price of the complete 302 HO engine package is hovering at $1,200 (before introduction time), but it could go higher because Ford is now talking more content. The engineers are contemplating changing the clearance-only hood scoop into a functional cold-air induction system. This would drive the price up slightly but would offer 10-15 additional horsepower under ideal conditions. That's pretty inexpensive horsepower.

Of course, there are still mileage considerations to meet, even in a new era of high-performance thinking, marketing and product; but the preliminary numbers look quite good. The 302 HO in a Mustang GT, at an inflated test weight of over 3,300 pounds, is expected to get 18/28-mpg EPA City/Highway numbers, well out of gas-guzzler territory.

Whether the Mustang 302 HO will start a new round of Detroit supercar wars is another question. It is a vastly improved automobile that goes, stops and handles well enough to outperform many of its more expensive competitiors, both import and domestic. And at a price that mere mortals can afford. For our money, it's the best-balanced, most capable Mustang ever done.

ROAD TEST DATA
Mustang GT 302 HO

☑ SPECIFICATIONS

GENERAL

Vehicle type	Front-engine, rear-drive, 4-pass., 3-door hatchback
Options on test car	302 V-8 engine, TRX wheels, tires, suspension, Recaro seats, AM/FM stereo, A/C, SS package
Price as tested	$11,000 (est.)

ENGINE

Type	V-8, water cooled, cast iron block and heads, 5 main bearings
Bore & stroke	4.00 x 3.00 in.
Displacement	302 cu. in. (5.0 liters)
Compression ratio	8.4:1
Fuel system	2-bbl carburetor
Recommended fuel	Unleaded
Emission control	Federal
Valve gear	Overhead valves
Horsepower (SAE net)	160 at 4,200 rpm
Torque (lb.-ft., SAE net)	247 at 2,400 rpm
Power-to-weight ratio	20.7 lb./hp

DRIVETRAIN

Transmission	4-speed overdrive manual
Final drive ratio	3.08:1

DIMENSIONS

Wheelbase	100.4 in.
Track, F/R	56.6/57.0 in.
Length	179.1 in.
Width	67.4 in.
Height	51.4 in.
Ground clearance	5.7 in.

Max. load length w/rear seat(s) folded down	66 in.
Curb weight	3,319 lb.
Weight distribution, F/R	58/42%

CAPACITIES

Fuel	15.4 gals.
Crankcase	4.0 qts.
Cooling system	13.4 qts.
Trunk	10.0/32.7 cu. ft.

SUSPENSION

Front	Modified MacPherson struts, coil springs, hydraulic shocks, stabilizer bar
Rear	Four-link, coil springs, hydraulic shocks, stabilizer bar

STEERING

Type	Rack and pinion, power assist
Turns lock-to-lock	3.05
Turning circle, curb-to-curb	36.6 ft.

BRAKES

Front	9.31-in. discs, power assist
Rear	9-in. drums, power assist

WHEELS AND TIRES

Wheel size	15.35 x 5.9 in.
Wheel type	Forged aluminum
Tire make and size	Michelin TRX 190/65R390
Tire type	Steel-belted radial
Recommended pressure (psi), F/R	35/35

☑ TEST RESULTS

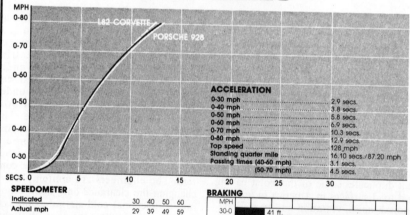

ACCELERATION

0-30 mph	2.9 secs.
0-40 mph	3.8 secs.
0-50 mph	5.8 secs.
0-60 mph	6.9 secs.
0-70 mph	10.3 secs.
0-80 mph	12.9 secs.
Top speed	128 mph
Standing quarter mile	16.10 secs./87.20 mph
Passing times (40-60 mph)	3.1 secs.
(50-70 mph)	4.5 secs.

SPEEDOMETER

Indicated	30	40	50	60
Actual mph	29	39	49	59

BRAKING

MPH	
30-0	41 ft.
60-0	159 ft.

IMSA GT Confrontation:
Ford Mustang versus Porsche 935

A performance test of the two hottest GT racers in the old neighborhood.

BY LARRY GRIFFIN

The tidy shadows of the Lola T600 and other GTP entries loom up on Group 5.

SPORT

Kings may die and be succeeded, and eras may pass and be replaced by others, but few of either will be mourned as much as the last hot breath of the Porsche 935.

We tested a 935K3 in the March 1980 issue, and Patrick Bedard, who actually bugged out blood vessels with the effort of driving the thing, came away feeling that the K3 might be an even more remarkable accomplishment than the Great Pyramid. The car he drove belonged to the Whittington brothers, and it had won Le Mans in June of 1979, just as Germany's Kremer brothers had intended when they built it. At the time, the 935 was the undisputed ruler of GT racing around the world, a domination that would continue until early 1981. Changes in the rules and growing interest from other manufacturers have changed everything, now.

Lola is building coupes for the new, full-race GTP category—which is intended to encourage flat-out competition in the manner of the old prototype days of Porsches, Ferraris, and Alfa Romeos, and new versions of mothballed dreams are on the way from a half-dozen mightily muscled sources. Lola has already blown the gleaming patina right off Porsche's long-nurtured image of invincibility, and to make matters even more unpalatable to Stuttgart

and Jo Hoppen, Porsche's competition czar in the United States, Ford has flagged down the IMSA express and hopped aboard with a European-built, Mustang-bodied, flyweight turbo flyer that's already snagged two outright wins in this year's Camel GT series.

It would be fair to say that Porsche is "Hoppen" mad. After years with the rules all its own way, the German juggernaut is so peeved that its parts bins and support trucks have become suddenly much more difficult to find for teams that had been raking in glory since time immemorial.

Ford, on the other hand, is fresh back into racing and out for everything it can get. The quick way to fame was to reskin a suitable existing car and punch it into the winner's circle with as much fanfare as possible. Listen closely and you can hear the blaring brass all the way from Detroit. Put the music and the good spirits down to Walter Hayes and Michael Kranefuss, respectively the prime movers in Ford's reorganized PR department and new-in-1980 Special Vehicle Operations branch.

Despite its quick and encouraging success, the "Mustang" racer can't be much more than a stopgap against the

PHOTOGRAPHY BY ROBERT HARMEYER, JR., AND AARON KILEY

same GTP cars that have so incinerated Porsche's peace of mind. Still, with the GTP cars in their early stages of development, both the Porsche and the Ford are certainly capable of winning, and you should not assume that either is anything but incredibly fast.

To support this view, we offer this test of both.

They are very different animals, each deadly in its way. The basic Porsche 935 Twin Turbo is a well-known quantity: air-cooled 3147cc engine in the back, somewhat antsy handling all the way around, terrific brakes no matter what, and about ten zillion horsepower to convert to forward motion. Anything with 720 to more than 800 horsepower and a rakish bulk of only 2430 pounds is enough to send any but the truest of the Mad GT Bombers back into the fetal position. John Paul, Sr., and John Paul, Jr., are still perambulating around upright, so it stands to reason that, since they drive this particular 935, they must qualify among the hierarchy of the Mad GT Bombers. The baby-blue JLP Racing 935 is one of the fastest ever built, but far from the most expensive at a thrifty, home-built $110,000 FOB the JLP shop (via the junkyard where the shell was found). The secret to this car's fearsomeness lies in its tubular construction, which gets away from Porsche's usual unit-body forays. The Pauls have built a very rigid 935 that carries its weight lower than your usual 935, thus allowing the bodywork to cling closer to the ground, where it nibbles around the fresh edges of ground effects for production-based racers. The result is a 935 that likes its cornering more than most.

The new, pint-sized bully on the block is perhaps even more adept at twinkling its toes. The Mustang is nearly 300 pounds lighter than the JLP 935, an advantage allowed by the rules because of its much-smaller-displacement 1745cc Cosworth BDA engine; but it, too, is massively turbocharged. The Miller-sponsored Mustang, run for Ford driver Klaus Ludwig by Bill Scott Racing, also has four valves for each of its four cylinders, whereas Porsche's six combustion chambers inhale and exhale through only two valves apiece. The Mustang's tubular aluminum chassis sits well down near the ground, the whole body sunk to about Salton Sea level in order to lower the center of gravity and cut wind resistance. Ford has also made a substantial attempt to take advantage

Vital Statistics

	Miller Mustang	JLP Racing 935
price	$250,000	$110,000
engine	turbocharged and intercooled 1745cc 4-in-line, water-cooled cast-iron block, aluminum head	turbocharged and intercooled 3147cc flat 6, air-cooled aluminum crankcase, barrels, and heads
valve gear	belt-driven double overhead cams, four valves per cylinder	chain-driven single overhead cam, two valves per cylinder
turbocharger(s)	AiResearch TB04S	2 KKK K-30
waste gates	2 Porsche	2 Porsche
intercoolers	2 AiResearch, air-to-air	2 AiResearch, air-to-air
maximum boost setting	19.8 psi (race), 23.5 psi (qualifying)	21.0 psi (race), 26.5 psi (qualifying)
compression ratio	6.8:1	6.0:1
horsepower @ rpm	530 @ 9000 (race), 620 (qualifying)	720 @ 7500 (race), 800 + (qualifying)
torque, lbs-ft @ rpm	300 @ 6400 (race), 350 (qualifying)	525 @ 5000 (race), 580 + (qualifying)
redline, rpm	9000	8000
transmission	5-speed Getrag	4-speed Porsche 930
final-drive ratio	4.38:1	5.13:1
differential	85% limited-slip ZF	none (titanium spool)
steering	rack-and-pinion, 1.3 turns lock-to-lock	rack-and-pinion, 2.0 turns lock-to-lock
front suspension	ind, MacPherson strut, coil springs, anti-sway bar	ind, MacPherson strut, coil springs, anti-sway bar
rear suspension	rigid axle, 4 trailing links, transverse Watt linkage, coil springs, anti-sway bar	ind, semi-trailing arm, coil springs, anti-sway bar
tires	Goodyear Eagle, F: 23.5 x 11.5-16; R: 27.5 x 13.5-19	Goodyear Eagle, F: 23.5 x 10.5-16; R: 27.5 x 14.5-19
wheels, in	BBS modular, F: 11.5 x 16; R: 15.0 x 19	BBS modular, F: 11.0 x 16; R: 16.0 x 19
brakes	12.0 x 1.2-in vented disc	13.0 x 1.9-in vented disc
curb weight, lbs	2140	2430
weight distribution, F/R, %	50/50	44/56

f today's ground-effects technology by carefully smoothing the underside of the car, even to the point of enclosing the live rear axle, and by creating aerodynamic tunnels within the zany body. And they said only drag racing had funny cars!

The Mustang is a lower and wider car than the 935. Its lighter weight makes it more agile. Furthermore, the Mustang's front-mounted engine is positioned so far back under the windshield that it's effectively a mid-engined car with a much lower polar moment of inertia than the Porsche. This makes the Mustang capable of being easily squeezed into inadvertent holes in traffic. The Porsche, however, is restricted to more regimented handling behavior by virtue of its chassis layout. The Ford's smaller power output (depending on boost, from 530 to 620 horsepower) also makes it more drivable in quick-response situations.

As you can see, this confrontation is a classic in every respect, and we can only lament the fact that it didn't come to pass before the GT cars began to lose their foothold on the top rung.

Klaus Ludwig used to win virtually every German Group 5 Championship race in Kremer 935s before switching to the Ford persuasion in Europe, and now America, too, but the remarkable young John Paul, Jr., is the only driver to have sampled both recently. He did so at the joint request of Ford and *Car and Driver*. Ford wanted to see if he would indeed make a good running mate for Ludwig now, and if he could perhaps even replace the German in whatever effort Ford deems suitable for next year. *Car and Driver* wanted a full test on both cars and a chance to watch the much-discussed new talent in action.

We discovered something interesting in addition to adding two significant new sets of performance numbers to our burgeoning reference files. The Mustang and its fearsome-foursome little screamer of a motor, puffed up as it is by a single turbo while the Porsche has two, is capable of getting off the line *faster*. It actually enjoys a one- or two-tenths-of-a-second advantage to as much as 50 mph. But . . . from there up, the 935 begins to haul the mail: zero to sixty in 4.6 seconds versus 5.5 for the Mustang, zero to one hundred in 7.9 versus the Ford's 9.2, and the quarter-mile in 12.3 seconds at 136 mph while the Ford could turn "only" 12.9 at 127. The stopping capabilities were virtually

dead even, and the Mustang pulled out only a slight advantage on our skidpad.

As you look at the cars' specifications, notice the difference in rear suspensions (Ford's live axle versus Porsche's semi-trailing arms) and consider these John Paul, Jr., observations on the cars: "The Ford is a very nice car, very controllable. You have to be a little more careful with the Porsche. Just a little bit of oversteer seems to be the fast way with it, so what you're doing is steering with the rear wheels. Our tube-framed 935 is very stiff in the front, and this gets rid of the inherent understeer 935s have had when first turning in. It just digs right in. The turning-in capability of the Mustang seems to be very good, because it has so much of its weight on the front wheels. Exiting the turns, it's very easy to induce power oversteer, maybe because it's lighter in the rear. The only thing I didn't particularly care for was the brakes, but they seemed to hold up in the Norisring race. The pedal is just real mooshy all the time, like it's not 100 percent.

"The Mustang has hardly any lag for a turbocharged motor, which is very surprising. It comes off the corners

well, although it doesn't seem to have as much thrust as the 935, but when you back out of the throttle and then get back on it, the boost comes back instantly. In the midrange it makes up for the loss of bottom end, which is very helpful at a lot of tracks."

From out of the mouth of a veritable babe, the definitive word on today's fastest production-based road racers. They may be dying, but damned if they're going to rest in peace. ●

Car and Driver Test Results

	Miller Mustang	JLP Racing 935
acceleration, sec:		
0 to 30 mph	2.4	2.6
0 to 40 mph	3.2	3.4
0 to 50 mph	3.9	4.0
0 to 60 mph	5.5	4.6
0 to 70 mph	6.5	5.3
0 to 80 mph	7.2	6.4
0 to 90 mph	8.0	7.1
0 to 100 mph	9.2	7.9
0 to 110 mph	10.7	9.4
0 to 120 mph	12.0	10.5
0 to 130 mph	13.3	11.7
standing ¼-mile	12.9 @ 127 mph	12.3 @ 136 mph
top speed, mph	180 (Atlanta gearing)	225 (Le Mans gearing)
braking, 100–0 mph, ft	360	355
70–0 mph, ft	177	174
roadholding, g	1.26	1.20
typical racing fuel economy, mpg	3–4	3

BIG-BORE NOSTALGIA . . .

Ron Wakefield drives Ford's new Mustang GT 5.0 but finds little more than a passing tribute to a bygone era

WE AMERICANS, as you Europeans may know, have been deprived of performance for some years now. First it was the anti-smog regulations which strangled our engines, so badly in some cases that petrol powerplants acquired diesel-like power ratings. Heavy bumpers and door reinforcements required by safety regulations compounded the effects. And, starting in 1978, our so-called Corporate Average Fuel Economy regulations — which require every manufacturer or importer of new cars to meet a "fleet average" mileage that increases each year until 1985 — exerted a further depressing influence on performance.

So the European reader shouldn't be too shocked that the most powerful Mercedes models offered in America have a 155-bhp version of the 3.8-litre V8, that Porsche doesn't offer the Turbo, that Jaguar withholds the XJ12, or that today's "big" Cadillac powerplant is a 4.1-litre V8 developing all of 126 bhp. Rolls-Royce, quite simply unable to meet this law, pays a so-called "gas-guzzler tax" on each new car sold.

Not that it's impossible to offer a bit of zip; there are just a lot of things conspiring against it. Furthermore, until recently a certain resignation reigned among most car makers, whether American, European or Japanese: the public, so it seemed, had become more interested in miles-per-gallon figures than anything else anyway, so why bother?

Like all tides, this one seems to be turning too. A booming cottage industry devoted to importing "contraband" European performance cars has grown up over the past couple of years, whereby such otherwise unavailable models as 5-litre Mercedes, Ferrari Boxers and BMW 323i's are massaged just enough to meet the smog and safety laws (cars individually imported aren't subject to the fuel-economy rules). Chevrolet and Pontiac offer a fuel-injected 5-litre V8 in their new Camaros and Firebirds. And to counter the latter, Ford recently revived the 5-litre V8 in its Mustang and (US) Capri, tweaked to 157 bhp by a revised camshaft, larger (but still two-barrel) carburetter and opened-up inlet and exhaust systems.

Unlike the Camaro high-performance engine, currently available only with automatic transmission, Ford's can be ordered with a manual gearbox, albeit an extremely wide-ratio four-speed with final-drive gearing that gives fully 31.6 mph per 1000 rpm in top. But at 3160 lb fully equipped — including air conditioning, power steering and removable glass roof panels — the Mustang is light enough for the engine to deliver considerable urge despite the rather uncooperative gearing. My test car had all these options and more, including Recaro seats, a premium sound system, handsome forged alloy road wheels with Michelin TRX 190/65 HR-390 tyres and the specific suspension tuning Ford does to accommodate them; with all this it came to just over $12,700.

In everyday use the big — at least by current standards! — V8 recalls the "good old days" of amply powered American V8s. It has that smooth, quiet, relaxed sound we took for granted in the 1960s, augmented by a purring exhaust note that could only come from a Ford. Despite the stringent emission control and lack of fuel injection, the engine runs well under most conditions, although it stalled repeatedly after cold starts. Though a high-performance unit in today's American context, by high-revving European standards it's still almost a tractor engine, peaking at just 4200 rpm and delivering plenty of low-end torque; that's why it gets along passably with the wide gear ratios.

Get along it does: from rest to 60 mph in eight seconds flat and to 100 in 25. Given the limitations of Southern California traffic and speed limits, I didn't establish its top speed, but from the feel of it at 100 mph in third gear I estimate it would reach about 120-125 mph in that cog at 5500 rpm. It might, just might, even reach its power peak in fourth, which would be just over 130 mph.

All this latter-day performance extracts a certain penalty in fuel consumption; in mostly brisk everyday use the Mustang turned in 18.5 mpg (Imperial). This figure looks even worse when you have to stop for a fill-up at a trip-odometer reading of 200 miles: the Mustang has a ridiculous little fuel tank of just 12.8-gallon capacity!

Ah, but this was always part of living with the American Musclecar — the fuel tank was meant for a "base engine" and ordering optional power didn't get you a larger one. Another tradition was always poor traction; the heavy, torquey engine up front and a primitive live axle at the back assured that. Here the Ford engineers have bolted a simple little correction to the Mustang's coil-sprung rear axle: "anti-tramp" bars with rubber ends that contact the underbody trailing-arm attachments when the application of power and resulting axle wind-up would set the whole into a frenzy.

They surely help — I can't imagine how bad it would be without them — but still, the Mustang's rear axle is its least controlled component. On sharp uphill bends, for instance, merely applying the amount of power necessary to keep going causes its inside wheel, being dragged along by the standard limited-slip differential, to patter and chirp in protest. If more power is applied, the rear end breaks loose easily, and extreme caution is called for in the wet. Nor does the Mustang's power-assisted steering break any new ground; though a rack-and-pinion

Macho Mustang: but ergonomically the latest version of the musclecar still lags behind European rivals

system it is almost devoid of road feel, and miserably slow to boot. In objective terms, the TRX-equipped Mustang GT is capable of 0.735g on a 200 ft-diameter asphalt skidpad, a figure several modest front-drive saloons can match.

The view forward from the Mustang driver's seat is dominated by a big bonnet bulge that's only partially attributable to the engine air cleaner; to the right rear, vision for manoeuvring is limited by a wide roof panel and the right front seat's head restraint. Again, typical comments for a US coupé. There is some progress in controls; Ford have finally adopted steering-column stalks for some driving functions, but the wiper-washer stalk is so far from the steering wheel that you

can't use it without taking your hand off the wheel rim.

It all sounds pretty negative doesn't it? There's probably a vestigial market for this traditional, crude approach to the American performance car, and perhaps one should commend Ford for at least injecting this bit of spice into a mostly unappealing selection from the home car makers. But the injected Camaro Z28 — although with its mandatory automatic box takes a second longer to reach 60 mph — is a far better driver's car. And even Ford is working in a more hopeful area with a new 80-bhp, tarted-up version of the four-cylinder, front-drive EXP/LN7 coupé. The Mustang GT 5.0, by contrast, seems little more than a passing tribute to a bygone era.

Five litres of slow-revving V8 engine make for a crowded engine compartment, but US regulations keep the power output down to 157 bhp

GENERAL SPECIFICATION

ENGINE

Cylinders	90 deg V8
Capacity	4,942cc (302 cu in)
Cooling	water
Valves	pushrod ohv with hydraulic tappets
Compression	8.3:1
Carburetter	Motorcraft two-barrel
Max power	157 bhp SAE net at 4,200 rpm
Max torque	240 lb ft at 2,400 rpm

TRANSMISSION

Type	4-speed manual
Internal ratios and mph/1000 rpm	
Top	0.70:1/31.6
3rd	1.00:1/22.1
2nd	1.72:1/12.9
1st	3.07:1/7.2
Final drive	3.08:1

BODY/CHASSIS

Construction	Integral body-chassis of steel

DIMENSIONS, WEIGHT & CAPACITIES

Kerb weight	3160 lb
Wheelbase	100.4 in
Track, f/r	56.6/57.0in
Length	179.1in
Width	69.1in
Height	51.4in

SUSPENSION

Front	Modified MacPherson struts, lower wishbones, coil springs above wishbones, telescopic dampers, anti-roll bar
Rear	Live axle on angled upper and lower trailing arm with anti-tramp bars, coil springs, telescopic dampers, anti-roll bar

STEERING

Type	Rack and pinion
Assistance	Yes

BRAKES

Front	Ventilated discs, 10.1in
Rear	Drums, 9.0 × 1.75in
Servo	Vacuum

WHEELS/TYRES

Type	Forged alloy, 390 × 190 mm
Tyres	Michelin TRX, 190/65HR-390

PERFORMANCE

0-60 mph	8.0 sec
0-100 mph	25.0 sec
Lateral acceleration	0.735g
Fuel economy	18.5 mpg

Longest Day '82

FORD'S SVO MUSTANG CHALLENGES NELSON

The adventures of racing a prototype for 24 hours

BY INNES IRELAND

Fuel feed problems were a source of frustration to crew and drivers. Bob Negstad was not afraid to dirty his hands. Kranefuss got driving and drinking tips from Innes.

PHOTO BY JOE RUSZ

PHOTOS BY BILL WARNER

YES, YOU'VE GUESSED right. I received another of those nocturnal calls from R&T's Editor, John Dinkel. This time he was perfectly articulate and more careful in his choice of time to place the call. I was wide awake and clearly remember his words: "Are you a glutton for punishment?"

So, being a glutton for punishment of this type, I found myself again at the Nelson Ledges circuit on the *Road & Track* team ("Longest Day of Nelson '81," R&T, October 1981). This year I was to co-drive with John Dinkel, Joe Rusz, Bill Warner, and Mike Kranefuss, Ford's Director of Special Vehicle Operations. Our race car was a prototype Ford Mustang fitted with a 2.3-liter engine, turbocharged and with an intercooler.

As I indicated last year, this form of racing cars from the showroom floor, with a class for prototypes, is gaining in popularity with not only Ford, but Chrysler, General Motors, Peugeot, Nissan and Mazda giving their support to various entries which numbered 40. With the greatest respect to the Quaker State people who sponsor the race and the Nelson Ledges circuit, which couldn't have a more friendly and helpful bunch of people to run it, it has reached its capacity to hold such an event. Facilities are decidedly limited, the circuit too short and too narrow to contain so many cars running for 24 hours. And, for some reason, probably insurance, spectators are not encouraged to attend. A pity, because these are just the people who should be there to watch, because the race cars are for the most part, nothing more than street cars with numbers.

Ford Motor Company, which has always held the view that "racing improves the breed," openly showed its involvement by producing two Ford Mustangs, one for *Road & Track*, and one for *Car and Driver*. *Car and Driver*'s car was to be driven by

PHOTO BY TOM CANNELL

arious members of that journal's editorial staff, ably assisted by Glen Lyall, Engineering Manager for SVO, who had been in charge of development and the test driving of the cars. It is a brave move to come out in the open and do your development in the eyes of the world, but Ford quite rightly believes that by participating in such an event, it can compress weeks of development time into a 24-hour period, and learn a great deal in the process. The results will be incorporated into future cars for the ultimate benefit of the customers.

We ran into trouble during the first practice session, unfortunately just after I took our car out. The "low fuel" red light came on, and a couple of laps later the engine started to cough so I came into the pits. Because the tank was still at least half full, the system was checked over and some dirt discovered in a filter. However, this didn't cure the problem which remained with us throughout practice in spite of the fact that pumps, regulators and everything except the kitchen sink was changed and re-checked. We did discover that the engine would run perfectly as long as the tank was full so we had this weight penalty when trying to qualify the car for a grid position.

I was voted into the hot seat for this task and after the first session asked for a stiffer rear anti-roll bar to be fitted to reduce the understeer we were experiencing. Comparing notes with the drivers of the *Car and Driver* entry, I discovered that we were down on revs at the end of the straight, and therefore slower, and whereas they had 12 psi of boost from the turbocharger, we had but 10. John McLaughlin, Team Manager, said he would turn up the screw for the final session.

We all tried the car in the final and agreed that the handling was improved, being more neutral, the car quicker through the

corners and easier to drive. It was, however, less forgiving, which gave rise to some concern that evening.

I was able to get a comparison of performance in the last laps of qualifying by following Glen Lyall. In spite of the alterations made to our turbocharger, I still had just 10 psi of boost and out of the hairpin before the pits straight, Glen would leave me for dead, reaching 6200 rpm in third gear, whereas I could just scrape up 5800 rpm before jabbing the brake for the right-hander at the end. Taking this into consideration, I was quite happy with my improved time of 1 minute 25.49 seconds compared to Glen's time of 1:24:80.

When we returned for a night practice session, it was to find that the mechanics had discovered a faulty bearing in our turbocharger and as this was being worked on, our car was *hors de combat* for this period. When Glen was unhappy with the lights on the *Car and Driver* entry he asked me to take it out and give some advice on the setting. The two driving lights fitted in the front air dam were too low to be effective and the other four were pointing at the trees with hardly any side spread to illuminate the apexes of corners. What I did notice particularly was the greater acceleration produced by this engine compared with that of the *Road & Track* car.

That night I gave much thought to the way I had set up the suspension for I had broken the rear wheels loose on a couple of occasions and while this was difficult because of the tremendous grip of the Goodyear tires, it was a fairly vicious breakaway that was difficult to control. Furthermore, if I overdid my braking entering the fast left-hander, the tail tended to snap away which was not terribly amusing. Because fatigue and emergency situations are inevitable in a 24-hour race, a little forgiveness from

The Porsche 944 won as many expected. But the 2nd-place Camaro V-8 and 3rd-place Mustang V-8 finished close enough to be considered future contenders.

the car is desirable to avoid going off into the tullies. After further discussions on the morning of the race, it was agreed that we change the rear anti-roll bar for a slightly softer one.

John Dinkel took our car out in the warm-up session and then said he was pleased with the handling, adding that the engine did feel a bit better with 11 psi of boost. Now all we had to do was wait for the 3:00 p.m. start.

I took time out to wander around and look at other cars. Things were different from last year. Dinkel's name appearing on just one car. Folks must have seen him creeping about or maybe he ran out of paint. I was really delighted to see Augie Pabst, not having seen him since we raced together some 18 years ago. The bumper sticker on his Triumph said, "Why do the British drink warm beer? Because they have Lucas refrigeration." Bill Warner presented us with beautiful T-shirts. Mine proclaimed, "I taught Stirling Moss how to drink." Last year it was "drive," so guess what it will be next year. I didn't understand Joe's T-shirt until I was told about the last lap of last year's race, when his car was shunted at the very last corner by the *Car and Driver* entry. His shirt read "Designated Hitter." Joe thought "Hittee" to be more appropriate. Apparently last year someone criticized John Dinkel's form of dress and his shirt said, "Who wears short shorts."

In spite of my performance last year when I started the race a lap before everyone else, I was again given this honor. To be honest, it was one I could have done without, because an hour or so before the start the heavy gray overcast had degenerated to rain, further soaking the ground which was already swampy from rain earlier in the week. I listened carefully to the pre-race briefing and made a mental note: *Two* laps behind the pace car and then go.

The front row was headed by the Chevrolet Camaro with the Porsche 944 next to it. Third fastest was the *Car and Driver* Ford Mustang, while we were back in 6th place, although only about 2 sec separated us from the pole. With the rain now stopped, engines were started, drivers strapped in, and we were ready.

As the 2nd lap was completed, the pace car pulled off, engines revved up, and we got the green. Between the second and

third corners, the Porsche flew off the road in a sea of mud, so that was one less to worry about. I managed to ease past our twin Mustang and then got the fright of my life coming out of the long right-hand carrousel. There was a change of track surface at this point and it was just like driving on ice. But I sensed it quickly enough and managed to keep the car pointing in roughly the right direction. Next time around I passed one of the other cars to take 3rd place. Great care was necessary for at all the corners mud was splashed onto the track when drivers clipped the apexes too closely and dropped off the pavement. On one lap a corner would be clear, and then the next, covered in mud. Since it is many years since I drove in the wet in anger, I was being particularly cautious and as the circuit dried, I failed to appreciate this as quickly as those behind me, dropping a couple of places. First the *Car and Driver* Mustang came by, and it was followed by the Porsche, which had extricated itself pretty quickly from the mud.

Shortly afterwards, I had my moment when about to lap a Renault Le Car at the fast corner at the end of the straight. I was just about to go by when it pulled right in front of me and I had to stand on everything to avoid ramming it, changing down to 3rd. I was certain he had realized his mistake, when the driver pulled away to the left of the circuit, as I thought, to allow me past. Accelerating hard down the right, I couldn't believe it when yet again he pulled right across me, forcing me onto the grass. It was impossible to brake, so I had to keep going, slow up as much as possible when back on the track and then spin it off onto the side. I lost a great deal of time regaining the circuit and had to wait while a stream of cars went by as I was right between two corners just before the pits.

At the end of the first hour a prototype 4-barrel Mustang V-8 led from the prototype Camaro Z28, the *Car and Driver* Mustang, the Porsche 944, a prototype Datsun 280ZX Turbo, and ourselves, 1 lap down in 6th. We were hoping to do 2-hour stints, but after 1¾ hours my engine started coughing and I pulled into the pits to hand over to John Dinkel. We had a lengthy stop as the mechanics were having trouble getting the fuel into the tank and after John got going it was obvious that

PHOTOS BY BILL WARNER

we were using more fuel than predicted, a fact confirmed when the other Mustang did well over two hours without running out as we had.

It wasn't long before John was back in the pits with the low fuel light on and the engine coughing. We were back in the same trouble as we experienced in practice. By the 5th hour we had lost 53 laps on our twin which was holding 5th place and 61 laps on the Porsche which was now leading the Camaro and the Mustang V-8. While our tireless mechanics sought a reason for our troubles, changing everything they could think of, we drove into the night just filling the tank everytime the engine began coughing.

I took over for my first night stint about 1:00 a.m. and soon found that the engine was down on power. Having been cautioned to go easy on the brakes, since the *Car and Driver* lads had managed to weld a caliper to what remained of a backing plate, I found a line around the course that allowed me to keep lap times fairly constant at 1:28.00 with a few 26s thrown in. I stayed out for 2½ hours, but made three stops for fuel during this period.

At halftime the Camaro was leading the Mustang V-8, having covered 475 laps of the 2-mile circuit with the Porsche ahead of the Datsun Turbo and a Toyota Supra. We were miles down in 35th place and 334 laps while the *Car and Driver* chaps had blown an engine which was being changed.

Two of my teammates had been out in the boondocks at different times and in their efforts to extricate themselves the clutch suffered considerably, eventually burning out. We lost more time while this was changed, but still we persevered, taking our turns to push on. But all this was happening after I had returned to our palatial Custom Coach motorhome to have some sleep in the queen-size bed at its rear. As I lay back and put the lights out I noticed there was even a mirror on the ceiling. Wondering what that was for, I closed my eyes and drifted off.

By 9:00 a.m. the Porsche had the lead back from the Mustang V-8, with the Camaro 3rd. Their new engine fitted, the *Car and Driver* car was going like gangbusters again and only 41 laps

down on us. We were still struggling on, making far too many stops, our fuel feed problems defying the mechanics' efforts to rectify it. By the time I had my last drive about mid-day we could still just manage to run 1 hour between stops, the *Car and Driver* car relentlessly catching us up. I handed over to John again, who was soon black-flagged for spilling fuel out of the filler. There was some excitement as he pulled up for the car was found to be on fire at the rear end where fuel had spilled onto either hot discs or the exhaust pipe.

Finally Mike Kranefuss took his last stint which would take the car to the finish. As the minutes ticked away the *Car and Driver* car sportingly slowed up as had been arranged to allow the two prototype turbo Mustangs to cross the line together. It may not have been a triumphant finish, but at least both cars were still running at the end, thanks to the non-stop and heroic efforts of our mechanics. The most amazing coincidence was that after all the stops and starts, both cars had covered an identical number of laps.

As for our car, apart from the fuel feed problem, it ran superbly throughout the 664 laps that it covered. In my last drive I was able to put in lap times the equal of those done in practice and we had no trouble from bearings, gearbox, or final drivetrain other than the clutch that was burned out when the car was off the road.

Having been involved with Ford during the early days of developing the Ford GT40 which in its MK II stage won the 24 hours of Le Mans on three occasions, I was delighted to find that the Ford approach is still the same as it was then. Every detail of the weekend will be logged and studied, shortcomings and failures examined and remedied in detail.

And the irony is that the cause of all our problems was a modification to the fuel tank purely for racing safety, a ball valve system that stops fuel leaking out of the car should it find itself on the roof.

Without doubt competition is a shortcut to perfection and I welcome Ford's adventurous spirit in participating in this event. And if they think of doing something similar next year, I hope they don't forget where I live.

'83 Ford Mustang GT

1983 FIRST DRIVE

You will recall that earlier this year (May '82) a Mustang GT and a Camaro Z28 squared off in one of our periodic fights to the finish. When the vulcanized rubber had settled, we scored it a victory for the Camaro, primarily for its superior ability to get around corners.

But those cars were 1982 editions. What we're considering in this issue is the '83s, and based on what we've just seen at Detroit's annual new sheet metal bazaars, we'd have to say it's going to be a much closer call next time around. Because the 1983 Mustang GT, you friends of wheelspin, is only a click or so short of being downright—are we allowed to use this word?—awesome. Not only is Ford's unabashed bad boy snorting out even more horsepower this season—about 180 compared to some 160 for the '82 model—it's had a lot of attention lavished on its handling qualities. The result is a much more neutral, balanced package that's a lot more fun to drive, with throttle-induced oversteer readily available in at least three of its four forward speeds.

Just what kind of lateral g this revitalized rocket will generate is something we won't know until we're able to get a pro-

PHOTOGRAPHY BY BOB O'OLIVO

duction test car onto our skidpad; our initial impressions are based on an afternoon of fast lapping at Ford's Dearborn road circuit. But lateral g notwithstanding, just try throttle steering with your stock '83 Z28.

The big difference under the cosmetically revised hood for the new Mustang GT (and its Mercury sister ship, the Capri RS) is the Holley 4180C 600 cfm 4-bbl carburetor sitting atop the intake manifold. This supersedes last year's HO setup, which employed a Motorcraft 2150 2-bbl rated at 369 cfm. You'd expect more horsepower from a straightforward boost in fuel feed such as this, and that's precisely what the '83 HO 5-liter delivers: 177 hp at 4200 rpm versus 157 for the '82 engine. Torque figures are comparable: 246 lb-ft at 2400 rpm for '83, 240 for the '82. And the power gains have not been made at the expense of driveability. This is a wonderful engine to live with—smooth, responsive, civilized, yet always ready for the instant transition to snarling combat readiness. With powerplants such as the Ford HO 5-liter around, it's hardly surprising that the V-8 engine still refuses to die, OPEC or no OPEC.

But we spoke of improved handling to

go with the power boost. And we spo[?] truth. The Ford chassis engineers ha[ve] done an excellent job of tuning out t[he] massive understeer that characterized ha[rd] cornering in the '82 GT. This was accom[?] plished in part by beefing up the front an[ti] roll bar, .67-in. diameter compared to .5[?] in. on the '82, and by giving the car bigg[er] footprint[s]. The 1982 GT edition Musta[ng] sported 190/65R390 Michelin TRX tir[es] mated to forged aluminum wheels. Mu[s-] tang GT buyers in the new model year w[ill] have the option of 220/55R390 TRXs [or] 205/70 R14 Goodyear Eagle GTs, both [of] them offering a substantially better bi[te] than the 1982 rubber.

Cosmetic revisions are minimal. Asid[e] from the altered front-end treatment, r[e-] versed hood scoop (GT only), and red[e-] signed taillamps, the current Mustang sti[ll] looks pretty much like it did when it r[e-] placed Mustang II back in 1979. Th[is] means it's not as contemporary as its riva[ls] from General Motors, although that ce[r-] tainly doesn't keep it from looking goo[d.] As you will note elsewhere in this issue, th[e] Mustang will also be available for 1983 a[s] a convertible, and the good news is you ca[n] order the soft top with the hard muscle o[f] the HO 302 V-8. It won't handle like th[e] car you're looking at here—convertible[s]

arely match the handling of hardtops—but at least you'll be able to get the wind going through your hair faster than anything this side of a Ferrari 308 GTS.

Ah yes—the question: *How* fast? And the answer is going to be on the equivocal side: faster than the last Mustang GT we tested, in that May '82 shootout, but no more than heads up with the first of the current generation of 5-liter GTs, instrumented in Dearborn for our September 1981 issue.

The numbers we got with that first 302 HO GT, a prototype, were definitely of the eye-opening variety: 0-60 in 6.9 sec and 16.1 sec at 87.2 mph in the quarter mile. The production unit that faced off with the Camaro wasn't quite so spectacularly quick: 0-60 in 7.78 sec and 16.26 sec/83.7 mph in the quarter (still good enough to beat the Z28 by almost a half second, though). And the pilot '83 we sampled at Dearborn turned 0-60 in 7.19 sec, the quarter in 16.0/87.3. The bigger footprint seemed to help in getting the car launched,

but we'll have to wait for a production edition to get any definitive numbers.

The fatter tires helped in the braking department, too, getting the Mustang from 30-0 in 41 ft and from 60-0 in a very respectable 160 ft (compared to 178 for the car that challenged the Z28).

So how much will these and other tweaks be worth when we actually get an '83 Mustang GT on our own test track? Who can say for sure? But we can hardly wait to find out.
                                        —*Tony Swan*

Ford Mustang/ Mercury Capri

FORD'S SPORTY car twins, the Ford Mustang and Mercury Capri, enter 1984 with some significant improvements and additions directly aimed at tickling the fancy and the throttle foot of enthusiast drivers. A version of the 2.3-liter sohc inline-4 has turbocharging. Electronic fuel injection has been added to the optional V-6 and all engines except the 4-barrel V-8 now feature Ford's advanced EEC-IV electronic engine controls. There are also two different versions of Ford's small-block 5.0-liter V-8, and a mid-year muscle-booster package will include tubular exhaust headers, dual exhausts, higher-lift camshaft, forged pistons and wide-open-throttle alternator cutoff.

To contain all this power in a controllable manner Ford has also engineered a special handling suspension that will include gas-over shocks front and rear and a unique rear quadra-shock configuration that includes horizontal double-acting hydraulic axle dampers as well as the usual vertical dampers. Performance-oriented versions of the Mustang and Capri will also feature accelerator and brake pedal revisions to permit easy heel/toe downshifting with the standard close-ratio 5-speed manual.

Inside there's a revised instrument panel offering red back-lighting and subdued gray suede-like trim, and a new 3-oval-design steering wheel that also includes a new center horn switch. In the rear you'll find split-back seats for improved versatility in carrying people and cargo.

Without a doubt these 1984 Mustangs and Capris are the best ever . . . except for the SVO version, which we suggest you read after you've taken a few moments to peruse these specs.

Ford Mustang SVO

YOU MIGHT wonder why we'd have a separate listing for one model of the Mustang. Well, wonder no longer. The reason is that the SVO is such a special model that it needs its own entry just to give partial justice to all the differences between it and the other Mustangs/Capris. The SVO is the first offering from Ford's Special Vehicle Operations (read race group), hence the name. And anyone who appreciates the European approach to balanced performance has got to sample this car before laying out his or her money for sporting transportation.

The SVO starts with a special version of the high performance 2.3-liter turbocharged and fuel injected 4-cylinder used in the Thunderbird Turbo Coupe and other Mustang/Capri models. It includes an air-to-air intercooler for more power and greater efficiency plus a 2-position (regular or premium unleaded fuel) calibration switch in the console that provides the driver with fuel octane selection capability. This switch adjusts turbo boost and ignition so that the engine attains maximum power without detonation. And the turbo 2.3-liter includes a specially calibrated camshaft and an engine-mounted oil-to-water oil cooler.

Besides the much modified turbo 2.3-liter that produces 175 prancing ponies, the SVO includes 4-wheel disc brakes, Koni shocks, sticky Goodyear NCT radials, a 5-speed manual that's been massaged for easier shifting and power assisted steering that's been reworked for increased feedback and road feel. The SVO also gets a special aerodynamic treatment including a distinctive dual rear spoiler. All in all, it's a package that will have a lot of more expensive GTs shaking in their rubber boots.

SPECIFICATIONS

Base price, base model $7472	Engine ....2.3 sohc inline-4
Country of origin ........................U.S.A.	Optional.........2.3 turbo sohc inline-4*,
Body/seats ....2D, conv, 3D*/4	3.8 ohv V-6, 5.0 165-bhp ohv V-8, 5.0
Layout ....F/R	175-bhp ohv V-8
Wheelbase, in. 100.5	Bore x stroke, mm ....96.0 x 79.4
Track, f/r.............................56.6/57.0	Displacement, cc 2307
Length 179.1	Compression ratio 8.0:1
Width 69.1	Bhp @ rpm, net ....145 @ 4600
Height..51.9	Torque @ rpm, lb-ft ....180 @ 3600
Curb weight, lb 2855	Transmission............4M, 5M*, 3A, 4A
Fuel capacity, U.S. gal. 15.4	Final drive ratio 3.45:1
Fuel economy (EPA), mpg:	Suspension, f/r ....ind/live
Federal 21	Brakes, f/r ....disc/drum
California 21	Tires P185/75R-14
	Steering type ....rack & pinion
	Turning circle, ft.......................37.4
	Turns, lock-to-lock 4.1

SPECIFICATIONS

Base price, base model $15,970	Engine ....turbo sohc inline-4
Country of origin ........................U.S.A.	Bore x stroke, mm ....96.0 x 79.4
Body/seats..................................3D/4	Displacement, cc 2307
Layout ....F/R	Compression ratio 8.0:1
Wheelbase, in. 100.5	Bhp @ rpm, net ....175 @ 4500
Track, f/r.............................57.8/58.3	Torque @ rpm, lb-ft ....210 @ 3000
Length 181.0	Transmission...............................5M
Width 69.1	Final drive ratio 3.45:1
Height..51.9	Suspension, f/r ....ind/live
Curb weight, lb 3090	Brakes, f/r...........................disc/disc
Fuel capacity, U.S. gal. 15.4	Tires 225/50VR-16
Fuel economy (EPA), mpg:	Steering type ....rack & pinion (p)
Federal 21	Turning circle, ft........................37.4
California 21	Turns, lock-to-lock 2.5

*indicates model described in specifications

Mustang SVO

Ford's future-think GT car

by Kevin Smith
PHOTOGRAPHY BY BOB D'OLIVO

ROAD TEST

Call it Future Boss. The Boss label worked well on Ford's muscular Mustangs of the late '60s. All this car does is update that same concept, translating it into terms suited to a more sophisticated, energy-aware market. Two decades ago, who would have appreciated a little 2.3-liter motor with all that fuel injection and turbocharging stuff hung on it? And this thing called an intercooler?

Times do change.

With the Mustang SVO—the first product of Ford's Special Vehicle Operations—this nation's second-largest auto maker demonstrates where it believes high-performance road cars are going. And while the all-controlling electronics, high specific power output, and race-bred technology show how we'll be getting more from less

in the future, Ford hopes they will also attract some of the dollars going into the import coffers today.

After a couple of brief but intense exposures to the new Mustang SVO, including thrashes around Sears Point Raceway and Ford's own test track at Dearborn, we suspect the car will indeed have some real success against foreign nameplates, though perhaps not quite the ones Ford is calling its targets.

Balance was a guiding principle in the development of the Mustang SVO; balance and efficiency—hence the pursuit of horsepower through technical finesse rather than sheer displacement. SVO director Michael Kranefuss (who goes back a ways

with European performance cars) identifies BMW's 318i as the engineering and sales bogey. That's what mandated smooth, sophisticated, broad-spectrum performance. And the engineer-heavy staff of 32 at SVO has done a creditable job of creating a broadly talented car, working with an existing platform and a limited budget.

We have a hunch most buyers who have decided to treat themselves to a BMW are not the best Mustang customers. But the SVO's combination of advanced technology, spirited performance, distinctive appearance, and realistic price will surely intercept a few folks on their way to Supras and ZXs, and maybe pick off the odd Audi shopper. An American GT could do worse these days.

How did the SVO engineers do it? By cleverly banishing the more blatant flaws of a rather dated body/chassis unit, and

This fuel-injected, turbocharged, intercooled engine is the central character in the Future Boss story

concentrating on a couple of areas critical to how a contemporary performance car will be received. The budget would not permit a new platform—which everyone wanted badly—but the company did realize this car's tech-minded buyers would pay for good hardware that mainstream consumers would not understand. So the trick was in placing the expenses where they would do the most good.

Handling needed a major upgrade, in terms of both balance and response, yet ride quality could not suffer unduly. The Mustang suspension has been completely reworked. Spring rates and bushings are changed, Koni adjustable gas-charged dampers and anti-roll bars are fitted at both ends, and a total of four radius arms (two leading and two trailing) control the rear axle. Front wheel travel has increased by a full inch.

A new steering gear fills the on-center hole that has plagued Ford products, and is perhaps SVO's best single example of spending money where it will earn an enthusiast's appreciation. In any car, the steering wheel provides the most immediate tactile feedback, so this system must be right in a car that claims to be serious.

Large ventilated disc brakes stop all four wheels. And those wheels themselves put the Mustang SVO in the exclusive 16-in. club. The 7-in.-wide cast alloy rims carry Goodyear's German-made NCT tires, size P225/50VR16.

External body changes on the SVO set the car apart from other Mustangs (and everything else), but the cosmetic enhancement has a clearly functional air. Though the basic Mustang contours are looking more boxy and upright every year, the SVO people have managed to give them a contemporary look.

Most strikingly revised is the nose of the car. A new hood sweeps down almost to the bumper in the center, leaving just a narrow breathing slit to augment the air intake in the chin spoiler. Lighting clusters

include nicely integrated parking ligh and turn signals, and headlamps that w look a lot better when they are given flus fitting, styled lenses as now allowed t NHTSA. A pair of fog lamps nestles in t spoiler.

At the opposite end of the car is an a aptation of the bi-plane spoiler Ford fir revealed on the European XR4i Sierra; is likely the SVO's most distinctive visib feature. Though the spoiler's contributic is essentially cosmetic at street speeds, plays a functional role on paper by elim

nating aerodynamic lift and even generating a little downforce.

Other exterior items unique to the SVO are rear wheel spats on the rocker panels, a clean single-louver effect behind the rear quarter windows, and an asymmetric air intake in the hood. That scoop's offset position raised some discussion of aesthetics, but at least the thing serves a purpose by feeding air to the engine's intercooler.

The net aerodynamic effect of the SVO body package is less stunning than it might be. The available downforce at the tail is a clear improvement over the standard Mustang's lift, but in the end, the streamlining efforts cannot overcome the increased drag of the fat Goodyears. Ford quotes a drag coefficient of 0.39, up from the standard car's 0.37.

Under the SVO's scooped, sloping hood is the true heart of this car, the object of Special Vehicle Operations' major effort, and indeed, the central character in the Future Boss story: the Mustang SVO's fuel-injected, turbocharged, intercooled engine. From just four cylinders totaling a mere 2301 cc (140 cu in.) of swept volume, this techno-freak's fantasy in living metal delivers 174 hp, placing it among today's better-performing big-bore V-8s for sheer output.

That is, of course, exactly where it must be to make its point. What Ford is saying with this car is, okay, we used to get horsepower by dumping loads of air and fuel down huge cylinder bores, but the way to

do it now is with on-demand force feeding and sophisticated electronic management of a smaller, lighter powerplant. All of which sounds great, but only if the power is really there.

To be sure the power *would* be there, SVO engineers began with the most sophisticated engine in Ford's stable, then improved it substantially. The cast-iron, 2.3-liter OHC four's best prior role was in turbocharged, port-injected form for the Thunderbird Turbo Coupe, introduced midway through model year '83. Its 145 hp and decent running characteristics provided a good starting point for Ford's new-era performance powerplant.

In SVO guise, the engine is thoroughly reworked; the key difference is the fitment of an air-to-air intercooler in the intake tract, which drops the temperature (thereby raising the density) of the air just compressed by the turbocharger. There is also electronic control for the turbo's wastegate—more precise than mechanical devices—which allows the engineers to tune closer to the ragged edge for up to 14psi boost. (Similarly, a dash switch chooses regular or premium fuel calibrations.)

All this trickery serves up 174 hp at 4500 rpm, 210 lb-ft of torque at 3000, and 6000 rpm rev-ability. By contrast, the "old technology" 5-liter HO V-8 we all loved in the '83 Mustang GT produced 175 hp at 4000 rpm, and—shining brightly in the one area where raw displacement cannot be re-

placed—245 lb-ft of irresistible torque at just 2400 rpm. (For '84, the top-line V-8's output is up to 205 hp.)

Where the Future Boss engine differs most from its 302cid predecessors is not in the amount of power it generates, but in the nature of its power delivery. In the manner of the better turbo engines we've driven lately, there is not really any troublesome throttle lag, but that's not to say power flows out instantly at any speed the way it does from a big-inch torquer. The little engine needs to get on the cam as well as spool up the turbine before it can make lots of power, and that takes time. It does respond to the throttle right away, but the real forward surge takes a couple of seconds to materialize.

Positive boost registers on the dash vacuum/pressure gauge at about 2200 rpm under full throttle, and builds steadily to its 14 psi maximum around 4200 rpm, just before the power peak. From 60 mph (2700 rpm in 5th), there is adequate roll-on punch to merge into a lane of faster-moving traffic, but anything more demanding, like a pass on a 2-laner, calls for at least one downshift and early throttle application.

Vibration also distinguishes this engine from the V-8s it hopes to replace. Under load at high revs, especially, the 2.3 buzzes and roars through the Mustang structure with unfortunate vigor. Rumors tell of a next-generation Ford 4-cylinder that will

The SVO people managed to give the aging Mustang conto

incorporate vibe-killing balance shafts (as well as four valves per cylinder) and that should reduce the problem. Meanwhile, the SVO's cruise mode is made to seem positively serene by comparison with its raucous demeanor under the whip.

It does, however, run mighty well—not quite like the HO V-8, perhaps, but energetically nonetheless. We instrumented an SVO on a hot and muggy day at Dearborn, and saw lots of 0-60 mph times in the mid-8-sec range. What we considered a perfect launch produced the day's best run of 8.12 sec. The last HO Mustang we ran (All-American GTs, July '83) gave 7.43 sec. Quarter-mile efforts compare similarly: SVO, 16.08 sec at 86.0 mph, HO, 16.06 at 87.5.

Now the cars were tested at different times and on different tracks, and we suspect the SVO was running perhaps a half-second off its potential (a faint stepping effect in its power rise pointed to a fuzzy boost modulation system). But we still don't believe Future Boss can quite run with the old guard in a straight line—particularly now that the 1984 HO V-8 is making over 200 hp.

Raw grunt doesn't count for so much when the road starts to twist and twirl, though, and then the SVO's recalibrated suspension and 150 lb less front-end weight make themselves known. The car exhibits

plenty of understeer when pushed hard, but even so, it's vastly more accurate and better balanced than the V-8 engined examples. We always found a 5-liter Mustang overworked its 220-section TRX tires to the point of desperation—the fronts because of the engine's mass, the rears due to its rubber-melting torque. Fast progress over a tight road or around a skidpad too easily turned into a white-knuckle balancing act, with the front tires curling under helplessly or the rears lighting up and coming about.

Its combination of lighter weight, better chassis, and bigger tires gives the SVO a

much more tossable character. It generate 0.77 g on the skidpad (again, that was no at our usual test site in California), an even though we expected better maximum cornering ability, there's no doubting th SVO is the best-driving street Mustang th factory has ever produced.

A decent driving environment is part o the package, as it had to be to attract th auto-wise sophisticates this car is going af ter. New seats offer Germanic comfor (firm and good-supporting), the stitched leather wheel feels right, and there's proper left foot dead pedal. The brake and throttle pedals have been reoriented to allow heel-and-toe operation, and the link age to the 5-speed box was refined through considerable effort by Borg Warner and Hurst (after Ford threatened to go to BMW, word has it).

We can make no serious complaint about the control layouts, but must let Ford know that the clutch pedal seems strangely high, and that the angle of the steering column did not pass unnoticed. The latter exits the dash panel aiming at most drivers' right shoulder, and while the asymmetry caused us no discomfort, it was a hard thing to ignore once we had seen it. A little more time in the car would likely acclimate us to both these quirks.

Simplifying the instrument panel has left a clean, flat surface carrying the climate

controls, a pair of air outlets, a few necessary warning lights, and the six round dials monitoring water temperature, oil pressure, fuel level, turbo boost, engine speed, and road speed. That speedometer, by the way, has its scale of numerals stop at 85 in the agreed upon fashion, but unlabeled hashmarks continue right on up to 140. All you have to do is count lines.

Our test SVO was finished inside in a low-key charcoal scheme, as will every one off the line this year. It's the only interior color offered, and it looks good with the limited choice of body colors: solid black, or metallics in silver, dark charcoal, and red.

There's lots to recognize as familiar Mustang around the SVO, and that's reasonable because essentially it *is* a Mustang. But it's also much more. It's a widely talented GT car that does not take the blunderbuss approach to getting its performance point across. There are details that betray the constraints placed upon the project, but overall, the Mustang SVO is bold in concept and intelligent in execution. That it exists at all, and that Ford has created a department like Special Vehicle Operations, is reason enough to be pleased.

Ford president Donald E. Petersen stated at the SVO press introduction that his company "wants to be known for building driver's cars," and that it *will* be known as "the company that is moving the industry in its new direction." Future Boss is a pretty good start at fostering that reputation.

But we can't quite leave this story without mentioning an interesting complication that may be brewing. SVO's boss Kranefuss, speaking at that same press conference, said they refused a V-8 engine for this special Mustang because the consumer was "more sophisticated" than that. And he's quoted in Ford literature as saying, "Everybody knew (in 1981) that in five, six, maybe seven years, the 8-cylinder engine would be history."

Look around the ranks of hot-selling performance cars, however, and you know that the inelegant old V-8 is not dying on schedule. Ford itself has been upping the horsepower ante, and there are already whispers about the obvious: a V-8 HO SVO Mustang. We'll be the first to admit we'd leap into such a car with relish, but what would it do to Ford's and SVO's "new-wave" promotion built around the high-tech four? People will be less inclined to believe you've built a better mousetrap if you keep investing in old-style traps.

Still, that's a problem for well-paid executives to hammer out. Devotees of tantalizing hardware and swift driving can just enjoy Future Boss for what it is: a symbol of where Ford is allowing progressive engineering to lead it, and another milestone along the high-performance automobile's comeback trail. 〔MT〕

Mustang SVO
☑ SPECIFICATIONS

GENERAL
Vehicle mfr.	Ford Motor Co., Dearborn, Mich.
Body type	4-pass., 2-door hatchback coupe
Drive system	Front engine, rear drive
Base price	$17,000 (est.)
Major options on test car	A/C, power windows and door locks
Price as tested	$18,000 (est.)

ENGINE
Type	L-4, liquid cooled, cast iron block and head
Displacement	2301 cc (140 cu in.)
Bore & stroke	96.0 x 79.4 mm (3.78 x 3.12 in.)
Compression ratio	8.0:1
Induction system	Electronic fuel injection (port), turbocharger, intercooler
Valvetrain	OHC
Max. engine speed	6000 rpm
Max. power (SAE net)	174 hp @ 4500 rpm
Max. torque (SAE net)	210 lb-ft @ 3000 rpm
Emission control	Catalytic converter, EGR
Recommended fuel	91 RON unleaded

DRIVETRAIN
Transmission	5-sp. man.
Transmission ratios (1st)	4.03:1
(2nd)	2.37:1
(3rd)	1.50:1
(4th)	1.00:1
(5th)	0.86:1
Axle ratio	3.45:1
Final drive ratio	2.97:1

CAPACITIES
Crankcase	4.7 L (5.0 qt)
Cooling system	8.7 L (9.2 qt)
Fuel tank	58.3 L (15.4 gal)
Luggage	850.0 L (30 cu ft)

SUSPENSION
Front	Independent, MacPherson struts (gas pressure), coil springs, anti-roll bar
Rear	Live axle, 4 links (2 leading, 2 trailing), coil springs, gas-pressure shocks, hydraulic horizontal axle dampers, anti-roll bar

STEERING
Type	Rack-and-pinion, power assist
Ratio	15.0-13.0:1
Turns, lock to lock	2.5
Turning circle, curb to curb	37.4 ft

BRAKES
Front	10.9-in. internally ventilated discs, power assist
Rear	11.2-in. internally ventilated discs
Swept area	432.0 sq in.

WHEELS AND TIRES
Wheel size	16 x 7 in.
Wheel type	Cast aluminum
Tire size	225/50VR16
Tire mfr. & model	Goodyear NCT (European)
Tire construction	Steel-belted radial

DIMENSIONS
Curb weight	1379.1 kg (3041 lb)
Weight distribution (%), f/r	59/41
Wheelbase	2552 mm (100.5 in.)
Overall length	4597 mm (181.0 in.)
Overall width	1754 mm (69.1 in.)
Overall height	1319 mm (51.9 in.)
Track, f/r	1468/1481 mm (57.8/58.3 in.)
Min. ground clearance	122 mm (4.8 in.)

CALCULATED DATA
Power-to-weight ratio	17.5 lb/hp
Brake swept area to weight ratio	284 sq in./ton
Speed per 1000 rpm in top gear	23.5 mph
Top speed	130 mph (est.)
Drag coefficient	0.39

SKIDPAD
Lateral acceleration	0.77 g

FUEL ECONOMY
EPA rating, city/hwy.	21/32 (est.)

☑ TEST RESULTS

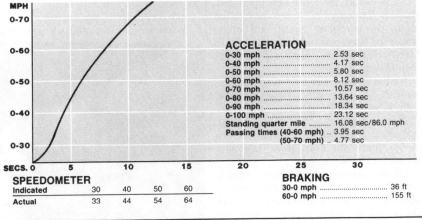

ACCELERATION
0-30 mph	2.53 sec
0-40 mph	4.17 sec
0-50 mph	5.80 sec
0-60 mph	8.12 sec
0-70 mph	10.57 sec
0-80 mph	13.64 sec
0-90 mph	18.34 sec
0-100 mph	23.12 sec
Standing quarter mile	16.08 sec/86.0 mph
Passing times (40-60 mph)	3.95 sec
(50-70 mph)	4.77 sec

SPEEDOMETER
Indicated	30	40	50	60
Actual	33	44	54	64

BRAKING
30-0 mph	36 ft
60-0 mph	155 ft

Ford Mustang SVO

Good news travels fast.

• Forty thousand feet. Ground speed, 545 mph. We are boring through the atmosphere eastward, ensconced in the leather-lined lap of luxury in one of the Ford Motor Company's Grumman Gulfstream corporate jets—which looks like a chopped-and-channeled Boeing 727. This is the rarefied air of the corporate giants, and sitting across the linen-covered table from us in a high-backed captain's chair is Ford president Donald Petersen.

We have lunched on cold poached salmon with dill sauce, green fettuccine salad with lobster dressing, warm croissants, California chardonnay, and chocolate-and-pistachio torte. Way up here, above the clouds, life at the Ford Motor Company seems very good indeed.

On the ground, though, things are considerably more tense for Ford. The nation's fifth-largest corporation has been doing well in Europe recently, but North

American Automotive Operations is fighting hard to stay profitable while attempting to close the gap on the Japanese. In fact, the company hasn't been under so much pressure since the fallow period in the early Forties, when young Henry Ford II stepped in to revive the organization.

We're winging our way back from yet another key new-car intro for Ford. What we've seen during the past two days amounts to the latest phase in the firm's revitalization program. Petersen officially laid out the plan on the first morning of the preview, in what began as a casual welcoming speech but turned into nothing less than a company manifesto. Petersen called for "a new functionalism" in Ford cars and the "ethic of continuous improvement." The goals are universally good: more refined powertrains, honest designs, more understated trim, better instrumentation, more thorough standard-equipment packages, day-by-day product improvement—in short, more of what we've already seen from Ford these last couple of years.

The past 48 hours have been spent in Napa and Sonoma counties—Northern California wine country—at one of the most gala press previews in some time. Headquarters was the posh Sonoma Mission Inn.

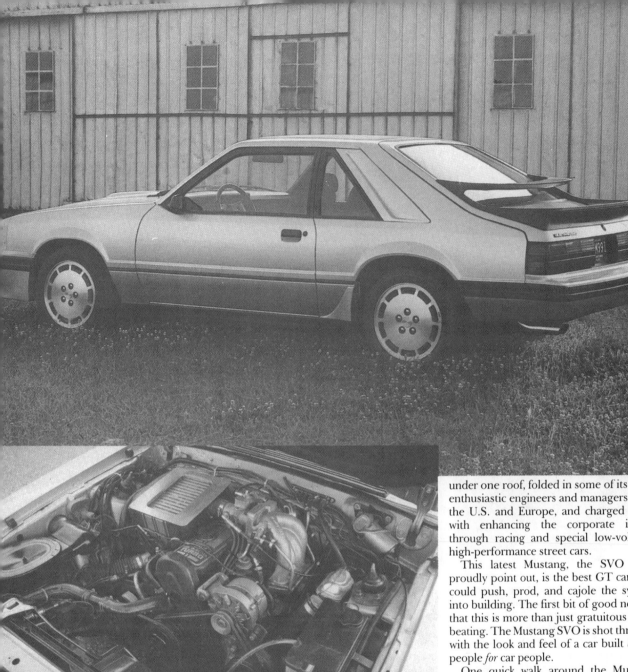

At the official unveiling, the Goodyear blimp hovered overhead, champagne flowed, and the crowd pulsed with corporate brass, but the real stars of the event were the new Continental Mark VII, which we sampled two months ago, a new turbocharged version of the EXP coupe, reviewed elsewhere in this issue, and the new Mustang SVO, the subject of this report.

If the thought of yet another permutation of the aging pony car is enough to elicit a yawn, we advise you not to turn the page just yet. For car enthusiasts, this is an important vehicle, a harbinger of things to come. The initials "SVO" on the rear deck stand for Special Vehicle Operations, Ford's racing division. This is their first baby, and it's a Mustang with a mission. During our lunch in the clouds, Petersen

described it as "our most definitive effort on the American scene to put together the finest we have in the way of a smaller-displacement, higher-revving turbocharged kind of touring car."

The Mustang SVO is a clear attempt to gain credibility with hard-core enthusiasts—you know, those souls who stretch the budget to buy an Audi, the up-scale trend setters and neighborhood car experts who can be instrumental in helping remake a car company's image.

Shouldering into the high-class GT arena is no small order—especially when you're starting with a car that's six years old. To make matters even more difficult, Ford had to invent SVO before SVO could develop its Mustang. Only three years ago Ford pulled its racing activities together

under one roof, folded in some of its most enthusiastic engineers and managers from the U.S. and Europe, and charged them with enhancing the corporate image through racing and special low-volume, high-performance street cars.

This latest Mustang, the SVO folks proudly point out, is the best GT car they could push, prod, and cajole the system into building. The first bit of good news is that this is more than just gratuitous chest beating. The Mustang SVO is shot through with the look and feel of a car built *by* car people *for* car people.

One quick walk around the Mustang SVO will convince you that it looks the part of a purposeful road car. It squats like a bulldog on the fattest rubber ever squeezed under a Mustang fender well: 225/50VR-l6 European Goodyear NCT tires on 7.0-by-16-inch alloy wheels. The new nose job isn't breathtaking—it begs for flush headlamps, which will probably come in 1985—but you won't mistake it for anything else, either. The hood has sprouted a functional, offset scoop, and the rear deck is distinguished by a biplane rear spoiler that adds a significant amount of downforce without increasing drag. (The Mustang SVO's Cd remains about the same as that of the base Mustang, however, at 0.39.) All of this is wrapped in a simple, classy one-tone paint job—your choice of charcoal, black, red, or silver—delightfully free of stick-on graffiti.

There's nothing to offend your sensibilities inside the cabin, either—just the most tasteful interior ever sewn into a Mustang.

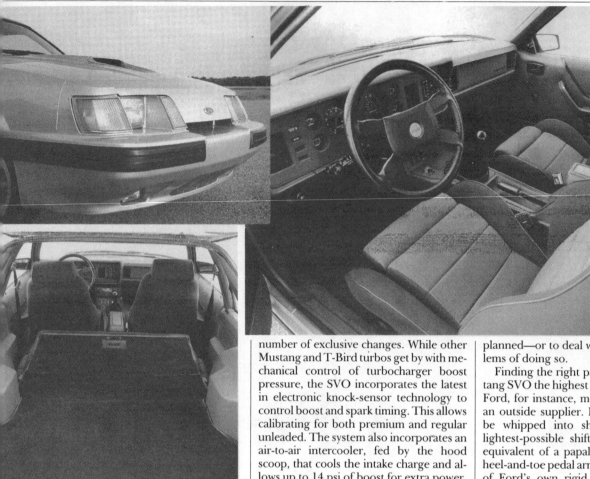

Deeply pocketed buckets with pump-up lumbar supports, a handsome three-hole Ghia show-car steering wheel (unfortunately not on our photo car), a leather-covered shift boot and knob, and attractive perforated cloth or leather upholstery give you that rich feeling. The only sour note is sounded by the standard-issue Mustang dash, which at least is covered in a handsome charcoal facing and offers full instrumentation, including a boost gauge.

Even the speedometer has been treated to the rebellious SVO touch. Because of a deal with the feds, Ford's lawyers wouldn't allow SVO to install an honest 140-mph unit, but SVO put one in anyway—without numerals above 85 mph. Your local art-supply store can help you finish the job with press-on digits.

Basically, though, the SVO's appearance is plenty good enough to rev up the heartstrings of car enthusiasts, so you'll be pleased to hear that an honest attempt has been made to fortify it mechanically for its new role in life. All Mustang SVOs start out as three-door coupes with 2.3-liter turbocharged four-cylinder powerplants. SVO, in attempting to take the Mustang to higher ground, massages almost every important component to some degree.

The engine, for instance, benefits from a number of exclusive changes. While other Mustang and T-Bird turbos get by with mechanical control of turbocharger boost pressure, the SVO incorporates the latest in electronic knock-sensor technology to control boost and spark timing. This allows calibrating for both premium and regular unleaded. The system also incorporates an air-to-air intercooler, fed by the hood scoop, that cools the intake charge and allows up to 14 psi of boost for extra power. The latest Ford estimate is that all of this good stuff puts about 176 hp under your foot, which places it in the ballpark with the 1983 Mustang GT's 4.9-liter V-8. Good mileage is also part of the deal; Ford expects an EPA rating of 21 mpg city, 32 mpg highway.

New goals had been set for the suspension, as well as for the engine. The changes focus on crisper handling and better steering feel, combined with a more supple ride than you'll find in the garden-variety pony car. To that end, SVO developed a new front suspension that uses Lincoln Continental forged lower control arms and adjustable Koni low-pressure gas-filled shocks. The springs, the bushings, and the anti-sway bar are specifically tuned for this model. The new pieces provide an additional inch of bump-absorbing travel for the front end. At the rear, the standard Mustang four-link arrangement is carried over with new bushings, springs, gas-filled Konis, and a pair of ventilated disc brakes for better stopping power.

During the course of the project, the SVO team's idealism was tested time and again by the inertia of a system in which, according to one SVO insider, "people are used to doing things the simplest and least expensive way." Like most big carmakers, Ford isn't geared to produce limited-production, high-performance models—a run of only about ten thousand SVOs is planned—or to deal with the special problems of doing so.

Finding the right parts to give the Mustang SVO the highest steering effort of any Ford, for instance, meant going to TRW, an outside supplier. Borg-Warner had to be whipped into shape to supply the lightest-possible shift effort. It took the equivalent of a papal edict to permit the heel-and-toe pedal arrangement in the face of Ford's own rigid passenger-car standards, which were designed to prevent the pedals from being too close for ancient safety reasons.

From what we've seen of the Mustang SVO so far, all the feathers ruffled along the way were ruffled for a good cause. Unfortunately, because of the constraints of such new-car previews, we had less than an hour of wheel time in the real world and only a couple of hot laps around the Sears Point road course. But we have come away thinking that the Mustang SVO has the unmistakable shimmer of a driver's car about it. When you strap it on, it feels right. The controls move with the heft and accuracy associated with some of the higher-priced European and Japanese sedans. The seat of our editorial pants tells us that this car is good news that travels fast—and our instrumented testing confirms it. Zipping to 60 mph takes only 7.5 seconds, and top speed peaks at a satisfying 128 mph. What's more, the seats feel good, the shifter moves like a fine instrument, and the pedals make you look like Fred Astaire.

By the looks of it, all this racy goodness will not come cheap. The system might have stretched far enough to produce the Mustang SVO, but limited production still equates with higher costs. Though no final prices have been set yet, the word we get is that the Mustang SVO will come in at around $16,000—which puts it square up against some pretty heady competition.

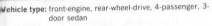

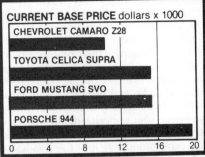

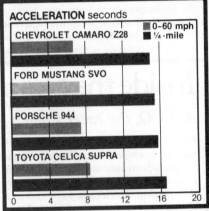

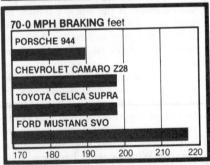

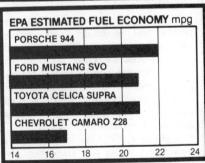

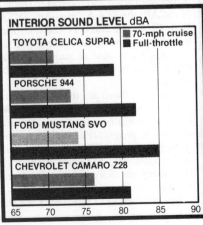

Vehicle type: front-engine, rear-wheel-drive, 4-passenger, 3-door sedan

Price as tested: $16,500 (estimated)

Sound system: AM/FM-stereo radio/cassette, 4 speakers, 12 watts per channel

ENGINE

Type . . . . turbocharged and intercooled 4-in-line, iron block and head
Bore x stroke . . . . 3.78 x 3.13 in, 96.0 x 79.4mm
Displacement . . . . 140 cu in, 2300cc
Compression ratio 8.0:1
Engine-control system . . . . Ford EEC IV
Emissions controls . . . . . 3-way catalytic converter, feedback fuel-air-ratio control, EGR
Turbocharger . . . . AiResearch T3
Waste gate . . . . integral
Maximum boost pressure . . . . 14 psi
Valve gear . . . . belt-driven single overhead cam, hydraulic lifters
Power (projected) . . . . 176 bhp @ 4400 rpm
Torque (projected) . . . . 210 lbs-ft @ 3000 rpm
Redline . . . . 6100 rpm

DRIVETRAIN

Transmission 5-speed
Final-drive ratio . . . . 3.45:1, limited slip

Gear	Ratio	Mph/1000 rpm	Max. test speed
I	4.03	5.1	31 mph (6100 rpm)
II	2.37	8.7	53 mph (6100 rpm)
III	1.50	13.8	84 mph (6100 rpm)
IV	1.00	20.7	119 mph (5750 rpm)
V	0.86	24.1	128 mph (5300 rpm)

DIMENSIONS AND CAPACITIES

Wheelbase . . . . 100.5 in
Track, F/R . . . . 57.8/58.3 in
Length . . . . 181.0 in
Width . . . . 69.1 in
Height . . . . 51.9 in
Curb weight . . . . 3102 lbs
Weight distribution, F/R 56.6/43.4%
Fuel capacity . . . . 15.4 gal

CHASSIS/BODY

Type . . . . unit construction
Body material . . . . welded steel stampings

INTERIOR

SAE volume, front seat . . . . 50 cu ft
rear seat . . . . 34 cu ft
trunk space . . . . 12 cu ft
Front seats . . . . bucket
Recliner type . . . . ratchet
General comfort . . . . poor fair good **excellent**
Fore-and-aft support . . . . poor fair good **excellent**
Lateral support . . . . poor fair **good** excellent

SUSPENSION

F: . . . . . . ind, MacPherson strut, coil springs, anti-sway bar
R: . . . . rigid axle, 4 trailing links, coil springs, anti-sway bar

STEERING

Type . . . . rack-and-pinion, power-assisted
Turns lock-to-lock 2.5
Turning circle curb-to-curb . . . . 37.4 ft

BRAKES

F: . . . . 10.9 x 1.1-in vented disc
R: . . . . 11.3 x 0.9-in vented disc

WHEELS AND TIRES

Wheel size . . . . 7.0 x 16 in
Tire make and size . . . . Goodyear NCT, 225/50VR-16

CAR AND DRIVER TEST RESULTS

ACCELERATION	Seconds
Zero to 30 mph	2.4
40 mph	3.9
50 mph	5.4
60 mph	7.5
70 mph	9.7
80 mph	12.6
90 mph	15.5
100 mph	20.0
110 mph	26.9
120 mph	42.8
Top-gear passing time, 30–50 mph	12.4
50–70 mph	9.1
Standing ¼-mile	15.5 sec @ 90 mph
Top speed	128 mph

BRAKING
70–0 mph @ impending lockup . . . . 217 ft
Modulation . . . . poor **fair** good excellent
Fade . . . . none **moderate** heavy

Front-rear balance . . . . poor **fair** good

HANDLING
Roadholding, 282-ft-dia skidpad . . . . 0.77 g
Understeer . . . . minimal **moderate** excessive

COAST-DOWN MEASUREMENTS
Road horsepower @ 50 mph . . . . 14.0 hp
Friction and tire losses @ 50 mph . . . . 6.0 hp
Aerodynamic drag @ 50 mph . . . . 8.0 hp

FUEL ECONOMY (projected)
EPA city driving . . . . **21 mpg**
EPA highway driving . . . . 32 mpg
EPA combined driving . . . . 25 mpg

INTERIOR SOUND LEVEL
Idle . . . . 54 dBA
Full-throttle acceleration . . . . 85 dBA
70-mph cruising . . . . 74 dBA
70-mph coasting . . . . 72 dBA

CURRENT BASE PRICE dollars x 1000
CHEVROLET CAMARO Z28
TOYOTA CELICA SUPRA
FORD MUSTANG SVO
PORSCHE 944
0 4 8 12 16 20

ACCELERATION seconds
(legend) 0–60 mph / ¼-mile
CHEVROLET CAMARO Z28
FORD MUSTANG SVO
PORSCHE 944
TOYOTA CELICA SUPRA
0 4 8 12 16 20

70-0 MPH BRAKING feet
PORSCHE 944
CHEVROLET CAMARO Z28
TOYOTA CELICA SUPRA
FORD MUSTANG SVO
170 180 190 200 210 220

EPA ESTIMATED FUEL ECONOMY mpg
PORSCHE 944
FORD MUSTANG SVO
TOYOTA CELICA SUPRA
CHEVROLET CAMARO Z28
14 16 18 20 22 24

INTERIOR SOUND LEVEL dBA
(legend) 70-mph cruise / Full-throttle
TOYOTA CELICA SUPRA
PORSCHE 944
FORD MUSTANG SVO
CHEVROLET CAMARO Z28
65 70 75 80 85 90

Still, with only 10,000 cars to sell, the exclusivity alone should create enough market demand to sell the line out.

Donald Petersen, you might be interested to know, was right there rubbing elbows with us press types the whole time—lapping Sears, drinking Michigan hummers into the night, and listening to our comments. And Petersen is one car-company president who understands drivers' cars, having just recently completed the four-day competition course at the Bondurant driving school.

As we begin our descent over western Michigan, he's talking about the highs and lows of the Mustang SVO. "Its special strength for me is its unusual blend of ex-

tremely good handling, performance capability, and ride quality. It remains a car that's friendly to be in, that's comfortable, that doesn't jar you." He allows that he would have liked to do a more modern instrument panel "that would have been

more compatible with the automobile." And he is vexed by our comment that the SVO drivetrain still lacks the smoothness of the BMW 318i that was along on the comparison drive. He's going to look into that, he says.

We'll have to hold off chiseling any of our judgments into granite until we see a production Mustang SVO or three. But we can voice our praise at the good news that Ford continues to move in a more enlightened direction. As Petersen says: "Big companies are like big ships: it takes a long time to turn them around." For now, we can all be happy that Petersen and friends at least have the rudder turned the right way.

—*Rich Ceppos*

Inside the Skunkworks

At SVO, the racer's touch goes in before the name goes on.

• For a number of years, Lockheed had a top-secret engineering group designing its high-performance military aircraft. Under the cloak of the strictest security, this division, which came to be known affectionately as the "Skunkworks," produced some of the world's hottest airplanes, including the razor-winged F-104 Starfighter and the spooky, matte-black, 3000-mph SR-71 reconnaissance aircraft.

You might say that Special Vehicle Operations is Ford's own skunkworks, the shop that's producing the hottest weapons in the corporate arsenal. SVO's official mandate is "corporate image enhancement," but that doesn't say enough. What we really have here is the *racin'* department.

SVO's mission is three-tiered: (1) to supervise and encourage Ford's involvement in motorsports, (2) to expand the high-performance parts program with more over-the-counter street-and-race pieces, and (3) to develop limited-edition, high-performance production cars that will carry the glory of the SVO racing cars out onto the street.

Right now, SVO has its fingers in almost every racing pie. The group gives technological aid and comfort to teams in NASCAR, the SCCA Trans-Am, IMSA's Kelly Challenge and GTP classes, sprint-car racing, off-road racing, and drag racing. Even a couple of showroom-stock drivers have been known to benefit from SVO largess.

And then there are the SVO production cars. SVO not only develops its own cars but works on other corporate passenger-car programs as well. (It was responsible for the EXP Turbo's engine and suspension.) SVO also orchestrates the movement of its cars into the greater Ford production system.

Yet another SVO function is the con-

SVO's new GTP racer: Think of this blue-on-white blur as corporate image enhancement.

struction of concept cars. The latest project is a Thunderbird PPG pace car, which is being used as a test bed for a new independent rear-suspension setup. If the results are good, the experiment could lead to more IRS applications in Ford cars, namely, the T-Bird and the Mustang.

All of this, amazingly enough, is accomplished by about 30 people. SVO is able to handle this load because it works on a cooperative basis with other Ford departments. In developing the new EXP Turbo, for instance, SVO tapped into the engine-engineering department for needed personnel.

Talking to the SVO guys, you get a sense that they regard themselves as a kind of outlaw band within Ford. A clear us-versus-them mentality exists, and there's a lot of groaning about "the system"—which they feel regards them with suspicion.

The ramrod of this outfit is a wiry German named Michael Kranefuss, who raced sports cars in Europe and served as director of motorsports for Ford of Europe in the Seventies. Kranefuss is not afraid to go to the mat when necessary. He chides Ford's manufacturing people

for "not being very flexible. All the time in a project like that of the Mustang SVO, you get people telling you that you cannot do this or that." Lately he says with a twinkle in his eye, "We are coming to a good compromise." The system is apparently bending further to his will of late.

Emerging as Kranefuss's right-hand man is engineer Glenn Lyall, a former Can-Am racer who knows how to push the right buttons inside and outside the company to get things to fall SVO's way. According to Lyall, SVO is beginning to earn the grudging respect of the old guard entrenched in the Ford corporate mainstream. "When we first started a couple of years ago," he says, "we were coming up with our own proposals. But now they're all coming to us and asking if we can do this or that."

Essential to SVO's ability to get things done is its speediness. A special SVO committee, composed of a handful of top-management personnel from the financial, manufacturing, engineering, planning, and public-relations arms has been formed to hand down quick decisions and to keep corporate red tape to a minimum along the way.

The biggest project on the agenda at the moment is an all-new front-engined GTP car. This is an international effort by SVO, Indy-car designer Bob Riley, and the Zakspeed folks in Europe—and it's being funded and constructed under SVO's auspices. The GTP race car will be followed by a prototype SVO version of the Mark VII for the road, a project that will more than likely influence future production models.

Where all of this will ultimately lead is impossible to predict. For now, though, it's enough just to see Ford changing the way it lives. Better still is the promise for tomorrow: when better Fords are built, the skunkworks will build them. —*RC*

GM's Corvette may look the part but in many key areas, engine especially, it's an outdated car, shaded by the General's more significant Fiero (see SCW Oct/Dec) and now up against two new turbo-muscled Fords for road and track that give the clearest indication yet of the musclecar's future

Ford's fantastic plastic racer

Ford's new IMSA challenger, the Mustang GTP, can legitimately claim to be the nearest thing yet to a plastic racing car. Its chassis and body are made entirely of plastics and carbon fibre, to give low weight and torsional stiffness — Ford says the GTP is probably the strongest racing car ever built. Light weight, too, is one of the car's key features. The amount of ferrous metal has been kept to a minimum, replaced in many engine and drivetrain components by aluminium and titanium. And yet for all this high technology — and the enormous cash investment it represents — the GTP is a front engine/rear drive car, a layout which at once puts it at odds with most of the world's road racers.

It's clear, however, that this car goes further than anything else from Ford and is laying the ground rules of the company's future sports cars for both road and track. The GTP also, of course, gives Ford something to shout about at a time when the General is grabbing the headlines with the Corvette and Fiero.

Ford US makes bold claims for the GTP It says the car is the most advanced road racer ever designed in America; that its computer-aided design chassis utilises the latest spacecraft technology (via Ford's Aerospace division); that its aerodynamics, with ground effects underbelly, draws heavily on experience with Ford's low drag prototype, the Probe IV; and that the GTP's engine is considered, by no less a person than Philip Caldwell, Ford chairman, to be the "most technically

Light weight, strength and easy repairability are claimed benefits of GTP's plastics/ carbon fibre body and suspension. Mechanical layout belies car's innovation: GTP is front engine (electronically turbo'ed 2.1 litre four, and rear drive, at odds with most IMSA racers but already successful on the track

sophisticated Ford engine now in production." Indeed, one of the most remarkable things about the GTP is the extent to which only Ford technology has been used — even the glass, with a windscreen just 5.3 mm thick designed to cope with speeds of up to 320 km/h, was formulated and manufactured by Ford's Technical Glass Centre.

The GTP project was directed by Michael Kranefuss, head of Ford's Special Vehicle Operations, and the car was designed by SVO's Bob Riley. Says Riley: "None of the individual elements of the Mustang GTP is unique, but the car's overall concept — a front-engined, ground effects race car — has never been tried before." The GTP will certainly stand out in the US's IMSA GT races, for it will be up against mostly mid-engined cars that can call on V6 or V8 power — very different to the 2.1 litre turbocharged four that is due to debut in the GTP at the start of 1984.

The engine is a smaller capacity version of the 2.3 litre four used in the Mustang SVO road car. It is turbocharged and controlled by Ford's EEC-IV electronic engine control system, and it should produce in excess of the 448 kW last year's 1.7 litre turbo four gave the GTP in its first outings.

Ford claims the GTP is two to three times torsionally stiffer than conventional road racing cars, as well as being easy to work on in the field: the 13 major panels in the GTP's chassis, which in bare form weighs a super-light 45 kg, can be changed left to right, for instance, because of the design's symmetrical layout.

Project chief Kranefuss says: "Because of the way the GTP is designed —

with a four-cylinder engine, turbocharging, electronic fuel injection, and an emphasis on aerodynamics and handling instead of brute power — we are making a statement about the direction Ford is heading with its future products. We chose a front engine/rear drive layout because Ford doesn't make rear-engined cars and we wanted to show that you don't have to adopt exotic configurations if you do your homework. The secret in race-car design is to get an ideal 50-50 weight distribution, a stiff body and good aerodynamics. We believe we can accomplish these characteristics with a front engine — maybe even get them a little better."

The GTP, Ford's first purebred racing car since the GT40-derived Mark IV of '67, is scheduled for a full year of IMSA racing in '84 — with Australian Geoff Brabham as one of the drivers — and talks are going on with Ford Europe competitions boss Stuart Turner with a view to the GTP racing in Europe. Kranefuss says: "If the car proves to be as successful as we hope then I don't see any problems if someone in Europe wants to race it." Is the Mustang GTP another potential Le Mans winner for Ford? Nobody's saying, but Ford do admit that the GTP is designed to be competitive in races lasting from three hours to 24 hours . . .

Mustang à la mode

Despite the reception given to the Mustang GTP, there were serious doubts in America that Ford's Special Vehicle Operations could come up with a worthy road car. After all, one-off hotshots for the road have to fight all

manner of bureaucratic dragons, not to mention the cursed 55 mph speed limit. The atmosphere in the US is not conducive to building the Escort Mexico-type car that distinguished Britain's SVO operation in the '70s.

And yet Ford US has persevered in its attempts to build enthusiast cars. The performance banner, until now, has been held by the Mustang GT, a factory hot rod powered by a five-litre V8 and, since last year, slurping fuel through a four-barrel carburettor. The GT offered

With 2.3 litre street version of turbo four and same conventional layout, SVO Mustang has at least something in common with its racing cousin. Performance is Mustang V8 good but price is half as much again: buyers will be more ready to accept SVO when unfashionably square body is ditched in '85

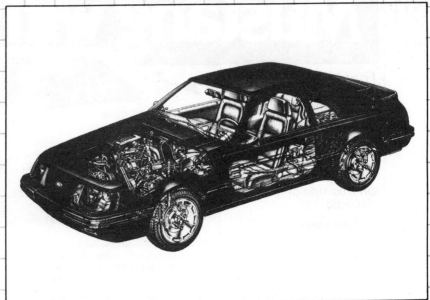

strong acceleration and some semblance of fuel economy when it idled down the highway at 55 in fifth. But it was still a gas guzzler — a 1960s-type solution such as a five-litre V8 with four-barrel carburettor can hardly be anything else.

Ford's performance banner is now held by the Mustang SVO, road going brother to the GTP racer and stacked full of 1980s-style technology. A four-cylinder engine in a hot Mustang may get the purists fuming, but it's hard to argue with the results SVO's dose of high-tech have brought: with its turbocharged, intercooled and electronically fuel injected 2.3 litre overhead cam four, the new SVO Mustang claims 131 kW (176 bhp), a very deliberate one kilowatt more than the V8 GT could claim, for about half the V8's fuel consumption.

In contrast to the usual American engine technology, the SVO's engine is highly developed. The intercooler, for instance, an unusual inclusion in a car of the SVO's price, is said to up the turbo engine's power by 20 per cent and its torque by 10 per cent, though actual outputs vary since the blower's boost is variable. Controlled electronically in a system similar to Saab's APC, the boost is controlled by an engine management module which also looks after ignition timing and, via a switch on the dash, compensates for different fuel grades. The driver simply selects premium or regular and the electronics do the rest — with the aim of preventing premature detonation. The system allows Ford to use up to twice the boost the company offered on its first, and ill-fated, turbo four in 1979.

The Mustang SVO comes with 'high performance' four-wheel disc brakes, rerated suspension springs, bushings and front anti-roll bar, a five-speed transmission — featuring a Hurst linkage, in time honoured Detroit performance car fashion — and 'extra feel' power steering. Not very long ago Detroit's car-makers would never use foreign parts in their cars, but the SVO takes a leaf from the Corvette book (which of course has Australian Girlock brakes) and uses some overseas-supplied components. The Mustang SVO's dampers are Koni units from Holland and the tyres are European Goodyear NCTs, though this will change later when Goodyear starts supplying Mustang-sized VR50 'directional' tyres, the rubber that has done so much for the '84 Corvette.

Driving the SVO Mustang is much the same as driving the Mustang GT except the tremendous opening thrust of the V8 is missing. Still, with lots of gearbox-stirring and plenty of revs to keep the turbo on boost the SVO's performance is much the same as the GT's, getting to 95 km/h in less than eight seconds, passing the 400 m mark in 15.5 seconds and going on to a 215 km/h top speed. The big difference between the two is at the service station: the GT with V8 is about 50 per cent thirstier than the SVO turbo four and that, of course, is what this new-generation Mustang is all about.

The biggest hindrance to the SVO's success is the styling — the design goes back to 1979. Even with the SVO's European Sierra-style double-deck rear spoiler, a deep front spoiler and rear wheel 'spats', this latest Mustang looks

high, square and old fashioned compared with the sleek Pontiac Firebird or Chevrolet Camaro. But since neither of these offers a turbocharged four and each outweighs the 'Stang by 180 kg, the performance/fuel economy ratio is inferior. A new svelte body for the Mustang is due in 1985 and then the Firebird and Camaro will be greatly threatened, but until then the SVO's rivals will continue to attract buyers for their looks alone, leaving the SVO to sell on its high technology image.

It'll be a tough sell. Projected price of the SVO 'Stang is US$15,000 and many Americans, weaned on big V8s, will not see the value when a Mustang GT with five-litre V8 costs US$10,000. Many buyers will look at the SVO and look at the GT and figure they're getting twice as much for their money with the V8 — however sophisticated the SVO's turbo engine may be. This is a shame for Ford since the company is keen to attract buyers away from V8s to high-tech — and, importantly, much more economical — smaller capacity engines. Cars like the Mustang GT, which attract cash penalties for not meeting Ford's CAFE (corporate average fuel economy) standings, are hitting the company where it hurts most — in the hip pocket.

Rarity value will help sell the Mustang SVO; Ford is planning a comparatively low 10,000 for the 1984 model year and that works out to less than three cars a dealer. The Mustang SVO may offer a glimpse of the American muscle car of the future, but it will look a lot stronger when Ford manages to ditch its still-bulky styling for a look that's more in keeping with its high-technology mechanicals. ●

Mustang with muscle

Ford Mustang SVO marks the return of something that seemed lost: the American muscle car. The techniques are European — but there are no plans for sale on this side of the Atlantic

By John Lamm

WHEN Michael Kranefuss (see page 36) was sent to the US to head Ford's Special Vehicle Operations (SVO), it was obvious the first vehicle that needed to be made more special was the Mustang. Once the darling of the so-called "pony car" class, the Mustang has suffered since its great Boss 302 Trans-Am winning days in the late 1960s and early 1970s. In succeeding versions, the car became first too heavy, and then too ladylike with the Mustang II. The latest Mustang, introduced for 1979, had the correct size and good looks, but something was still missing: excitement under the bonnet.

There was a badly botched attempt to produce a turbocharged Mustang early in its present model life, resulting in a remarkably bad car in which the turbo boost brought more noise but little added speed. It took the option of a 5-litre V8 two years ago finally to produce a Mustang that would once again get to 60 mph in under 10 seconds. That was better, but it wasn't good enough for Kranefuss.

As with the race car, SVO had two directions they could take with the Mustang. One was the safe, traditional route of producing a conventional car powered by a V8 engine. But Kranefuss, very well acquainted with the success of the German-built Zakspeed mega-horsepower, turbo four-cylinder Capris, preferred the European way. He figured that both SVO's IMSA race car and their Mustang would say a great deal more about Ford if they were technologically up-to-date, using small-displacement, turbocharged engines and, in the case of the race car, exotic materials.

It certainly would have been easier the other way, but the success of the SVOs has already proved him right. The race car won on its maiden outing and the Mustang has had rave reviews from everyone who has road tested it. American automotive magazines have pegged the SVO's 0-60 mph time at 7.5 to 7.7 seconds, and the car's handling, despite its live rear axle, is excel-

lent, without the teeth-jarring ride that too often accompanies decent handling from American cars.

The heart of SVO's Mustang is Ford's 2.3-litre in-line single-overhead-cam four-cylinder engine. They had already fuel-injected and turbocharged this engine for the 145 bhp power-plant in the Ford Thunderbird and Mustang and Mercury Cougar and Capri. The SVO turbo-four starts as that same engine, but goes a few more steps.

First addition is an intercooler that lowers the intake charge from 300 deg. F to 175, producing a denser charge. This intercooler is essentially the same as the three intercoolers used on the race car. Just as important is the EEC-IV electronic engine control system that takes a broad range of inputs and then juggles boost, ignition, timing and air charge for the best performance regardless of altitude or fuel quality. That fuel question is a open one throughout the US with high-octane unleaded petrol available in some parts of the country, but minimal-octane unleaded regular sold in others. The computer in the EEC-IV can allow for all these variations, but Ford also put a switch on the Mustang's dashboard to change the microprocessor from a regular fuel "map" to one for premium.

Under ideal conditions, the SVO turbo can wind itself up to 14 psi boost and produce 175 bhp at 4,500 rpm and 210 lb.ft. of torque at 3,000 rpm. With its five-speed manual gearbox, that's

enough to get the 3,200lb Mustang to 60 mph in the mid-7 second range and keep it going to a top speed of around 130 mph. These performance figures may be somewhat impressive to Europe, but to American enthusiasts they are a godsend. Remember that the States have been through almost a decade which American carmakers shunned real performance cars other than the Corvette and, to a lesser extent, the Mustang, Camaro Z/28 and Pontiac Trans-Am. The SVO Mustang and the new Corvette (and the Fiero, if it had more horsepower) are the leading edge of a performance revival that includes such turbocharged treats as the Chrysler Laser, Dodge Daytona and Pontiac 2000 Sunbird.

The front suspension is the

same modified MacPherson strut design used in Ford's front-engine/rear-drive models these days, but more deftly tuned and sporting Koni adjustable shock absorbers. The same dampers are used in the four-link, coil spring rear suspension. (Given the chance to make another major change on the Mustang it probably would have been to an independent rear suspension, but this model is somewhat aged. There are, however, experimental Thunderbirds with an SVO-inspired irs . . .) Goodyear NCT 225/50VR-16 radials are the standard SVO tyres and there are disc brakes front and rear.

The basic driving attitude of the SVO is nicely balanced and neutral. Driven hard, understeer is

the next step for the Mustang not the severe sort we've co expect from Detroit cars. Th is nonetheless very reaso for a car with the SVO's har potential. That potential w up during 1984 with the ad of two more dampers on th axle and the Corvette-type year Eagle GT tyres.

Unlike so many Detroit formance cars, which we flash and no substance, have kept the Mustang's ap ance changes to a few that ter. The front end is differe distinguish it from lesser tangs. The offset hood sc there for the intercooler. A back is a Sierra XR4i-style tier spoiler. The interior is up in matt grey, with a s dashboard that includes on necessary gauges, and seat hold you in place as the forces rise.

The SVO Mustang is, in t very impressive package sells in the US for under dollars (£11,000) equipped almost everything you want. That put it 9,000 dolla der the Corvette. It make wonder what SVO will be a accomplish when they can a new car.

Outwardly, the SVO is a Mustang with Sierra touches — like the bluff front and the XR4 bi-plane wing. Offset bonnet scoop channels air to the turbo intercooler of the four cylinder "Lima" engine (right)

By Kevin Boales

FORD SVO
DODGE DAYTONA TURBO

The Two Baddest American 4-bangers Ever Built

Performance Test

No doubt about it, when Detroit wants to build something interesting, they can do a great job. The "new" Chrysler Corporation, armed with the industry's largest resource of computer-aided design and manufacturing tools, is making cars packed with so much technology they're bursting at the seams, and Ford's Special Vehicle Operations (SVO) has embraced a mission: to design and build the most technically sophisticated cars in Ford's production history.

The SVO Mustang is designed to satisfy anyone with an eye for hardware and manic driving technique; it is a no-frills, high-buck hot rod that will spin both rear wheels anytime, anywhere. It has gigantic, four-wheel disc brakes, Koni adjustable struts and shocks, king-size sway bars, 16-inch cast wheels, and Goodyear Eagles.

Dodge began with a new car, significantly different from the earlier Charger series. This new "G-24" chassis is an exceptionally rigid, tight, and well finished piece of computer-generated sheetmetal. The Daytona and twin Chrysler Laser are aimed toward the person wanting a slick, fast, and well-mannered high-speed tourer. It is 300 pounds lighter than the SVO at 2651 pounds.

Under the SVO Mustang's hood lives a monster . . . by 4-cylinder standards. SVO's choice for the Mustang is a 2.3 liter OHC engine—the same basic engine that has powered Fords for years. Stubbornly rugged, the 2.3 exhibits a familiar rattle when the tach goes past three grand, and by 4500 you'll swear the pistons are going to swap holes, but the engine keeps on spinning. The SVO 2.3 is equipped with forged pistons to survive the real focal point of this engine: it is turbocharged, intercooled for a serious increase in boost, and has multi-point electronic fuel injection. If you had told someone 10 years ago that Ford would build such a car and sell it to Joe Lunchbox, you would

have been termed an incurable liar.

The 2.2 liter Chrysler OHC engine is proving to be possibly the most rugged four-holer ever designed, and fitted with a Chrysler-modified water cooled AiResearch TO3 turbo and multi-point fuel injection makes 142 horsepower. The SVO produces 174. Two areas may be responsible for the power difference: the SVO engine runs under heavier boost (up to 15 psi vs. the Dodge at 7 psi) and the Ford is a cross-flow head, whereas the Dodge has all the ports on the rear side of the engine. Ford's engine is equipped with electronic boost control, capable of maintaining its prescribed boost levels at any reasonable altitude. Next year's Daytona is rumored to be an intercooled model making 14-15 pounds of boost and an estimated 180 horsepower. If produced, it'll make driving the front-wheel drive car a spooky experience.

The Dodge interior is a different environment altogether from the SVO; where the Dodge is cushy, well detailed, and quiet, the SVO displays all the panache of a cafeteria tray. Of course, as we said before, the SVO is

for thrashing and the Dodge is for touring. Both succeed in their form following function.

Inside, the Mustang is Spartan, with excellent seating (except for lack of forward restraint, causing the unoccupied passenger seat to plop forward with every hard application of the brakes), a *perfect* steering wheel, good pedal position, and a shifter that is a little long in throw but smooth and precise.

The Dodge is as ergonometrically correct as the SVO, with a decent steering wheel, good shifter position, and reasonable pedal placement. Both cars have "dead pedals" to the left of the clutch; after driving a car with one, you'll be spoiled and looking for a place to rest your foot in any other car.

The Dodge does not have four-wheel discs, nor does it need them. With front-wheel drive, far more of the braking effort is exerted by the front brakes than with rear-wheel drive due to the forward weight bias FWD cars have. The Daytona is equipped with adequate front brakes (ventilated disc) and seems to have nearly perfect front-to-rear braking calibration. To contend with its greater horsepower output, SVO equipped the Mustang with big discs all around.

In the handling department, the two cars both shine, although in different styles. Driving a front-wheel drive car hard over a tight mountain road has been complicated in the past by torque steer problems and poor braking bias. Chrysler assigned the development engineers for the Daytona the task of minimizing these glitches. We already discussed the braking situation, and they devised a novel way to fight the torque steer problem: by installing a "pillow block" sort of bearing on the right-hand side of the engine block and using an intermediate shaft between the trans

Dominating the SVO engine compartment is the air-to-air intercooler, said to be about one-third the size of the one in the track-burning Mustang GTP car. Although you need to remove it to change the spark plugs, it comes out quickly with four bolts and two clamps. Once removed, the plugs are staring you in the face; so is the turbo-charger. The SVO uses a nifty oil cooler that fits between the oil filter and the engine block. Coolant is circulated through the casting, drawing heat from the oil and taking it away to the radiator. Compact and effective.

No frills interior won't distract you from driving chores. The SVO interior is, well . . . plain. Seating, driver position, and pedal placement are excellent. This car is meant to be hammered.

*To experience the SVO at its finest, try blasting your way up or down a mountain road. The neatest part is when you're within the engine's boost range, driving on the whistle; a little throttle yields a **lot** of response between 2500 and 5000 rpm. Fun, fun, fun . . . .*

SVO/DAYTONA

The Daytona uses a turbo of the same general size as the SVO, but the center housing is water cooled and the Chrysler engineers redesigned the cold-side housing, hot-side outlet, and wastegate. Water-cooling the center section more or less eliminates cooking the bearings during the heat soak period following engine shutdown. When Lee says they'll last five or 50, he means it.

Functional hood grille on the Daytona provides air for cooling the small engine compartment rather than to an air filter. Duct (arrow) squirts cool air down to the turbo and in back of the engine to keep your shoes from melting to the floor. The turbo is shoehorned between engine and firewall.

Yes, things are a bit tight under the Daytona hood. The engine compartment is necessarily well organized, and servicing this car shouldn't be any tougher than our Rampage project truck of last year. Normal stuff like spark plugs are a cinch. An improved belt layout also helps; the Rampage was **not** fun to work on in that area.

Quick steering, agile, and low, the Daytona (top) lacks some of the brute feel of the SVO, but will make short work of tight roads. This is perhaps the best handling front-wheel drive vehicle to come along so far, with carefully chosen sway bar and spring rates, a few trick bushings here and there, and a **very** fast steering box.

output and the right-hand axle, they made the two axles identical in length. The result was a compromise: the torque steer isn't gone, but if you put 142 horsepower into a Honda, it would in all likelihood be uncontrollable. The Dodge, as does any high-output front-wheel drive car, needs positraction. Small units exist that could be integrated into the transaxles, perhaps in the near future.

The SVO is the finest handling, most balanced Mustang ever sold, in our opinion. It is equipped with a Traction-Lok differential (which it *needs*), and the combination of shocks, struts, and other suspension pieces makes the car predictable and stable at nearly any speed. One of the real pleasures of driving this car is getting it slightly into the boost range and then driving it "on the whistle" through a series of corners. In 3rd gear, the car pulls from about 2500 rpm to 5000 with an ease that you should really experience in the hills. The turbo on the SVO is amazingly loud, causing all the dogs in our neighborhood to tilt their heads at the car's approach, making them look like Nipper, the RCA trademark dog of old.

Although we normally leave comments about fit and finish to our buddies at *Motor Trend*, we have to say something about how well the Dodge is assembled. It may have a lot to do with the G chassis design, but it's more likely due to direct involvement on the assembly line. All the body seams are perfect, the doors don't leak, and the windows open and close with astonish-

Would you believe this is an American, front-wheel drive, 4-cylinder car? High-style interior of the Dodge was really comfortable, and instruments and controls are well positioned. Boost gauge (arrow) is more prominent in the Daytona cockpit than in the SVO, whose designers figured you should be looking at the road instead of watching the needle swing around on the dash. Both cars had tilt columns and multi-adjustable seats with air-filled thigh and lumbar supports. The SVO seats offered a little more lateral support than these, but the Daytona seating is nothing short of first-class.

SVO/DAYTONA

Special mention has to be made of the astonishing quality of the Daytona body assembly. Seams are perfect! Now if only they can learn to shoot black enamel without orange peel....

Both the SVO and Daytona are admirable strip performers considering their displacement and design intention (high-speed roadwork). The Daytona was about a half second slower than the SVO, due to several factors including front-wheel drive, less boost, and a transaxle full of tall gears. On the other hand, the Daytona gets farther on a gallon of juice.

The SVO is equipped with Koni adjustable struts and shocks, and the struts are easily recalibrated with a tool supplied with the car. As with any Koni adjustable, a little goes a long way. The car can be made to feel like a kart, or can be fairly soft.

ing smoothness. Chrysler has made intelligent use of plastics throughout the car, but they aren't conspicuous, even up close. The engine compartment is well detailed—a miracle considering the amount of hardware crammed into the space. Wiring and plumbing are well routed and tied into neat bundles. Servicing the car should be a breeze despite the tight quarters.

Neither of these cars was designed to be a grocery getter or to age, neglected and covered with bird droppings, behind the trash cans in your driveway. They're meant to be driven—the SVO, to be driven very hard . . . the Dodge with precision. Both are fine examples of what Detroit can do when given a little room to play and an appreciative public. You wanted performance cars of the Eighties? Here they are! **HR**

SPEC SHEET

'84 Ford Mustang SVO

ENGINE:
Type..............................SOHC inline 4-cylinder, two valves per cylinder.
Displacement...........................2.3 liters (139.38 cubic inches)
Bore & Stroke.........................3.780x3.120 inches
Compression Ratio 8.0:1
Induction System ....Multi-point electronic fuel injection, turbocharger, electronically controlled wastegate, intercooler
Horsepower...............................174 @ 4500 rpm
Torque ....210 lb.-ft. @ 3000 rpm
Recommended Fuel ....Premium unleaded (calibration switch provided for use of regular unleaded; limits boost to approximately 10 psi)

DRIVETRAIN:
Transmission.............................Borg-Warner T5 5-speed manual, overdrive 5th gear
Axle Ratio/Type.....................3.45:1/Ford Traction-Lok

SUSPENSION:
Front ....Independent, Koni gas-filled MacPherson type struts, adjustable rebound control, 1.20-inch-diameter sway bar
Rear ....Four-bar (two leading, two trailing axle), Koni gas shocks
Steering Box Ratio/Type ....Variable ratio (20:1 at center) power rack-and-pinion
Wheels.....................................16x7-inch cast aluminum, five lug
Tires...225/50VR-16 Goodyear NCT

GENERAL:
Curb Weight...............................3035 pounds
Weight Distribution....................59/41 (front/rear)
Fuel Economy (observed)........19 city/23 highway
Quarter-mile...............................15.80 @ 87.39 mph
Skidpad (G)................................0.78

NOTES:
Our SVO came equipped with air conditioning, power steering, power brakes, and Ford Premium Sound System. Also available are a sunroof and leather seat trim. No other options offered at the time of this writing.

SPEC SHEET

'84 Dodge Daytona Turbo Z

ENGINE:
Type..SOHC inline 4-cylinder, two valves per cylinder, mounted transversely (front-wheel drive)
Displacement...........................2.2 liters (133.3 cubic inches)
Bore & Stroke.........................3.44x3.62 inches
Compression Ratio ....8:1 (turbo version only)
Induction System ....Multi-point electronic fuel injection; water-cooled turbocharger
Horsepower...............................142 @ 5600 rpm
Torque ....160 lb.-ft. @ 3200 rpm
Recommended Fuel ....Premium unleaded (engine is equipped with a detonation sensor which recalibrates engine controls if lower octane fuels are used)

DRIVETRAIN:
Transmission.............................5-speed manual transaxle; 5th gear is overdrive
Axle Ratio/Type.....................3.56:1/open type

SUSPENSION:
Front ....Independent, front wheels are driven, modified MacPherson strut suspension utilizing "Iso-strut" design (dual-path shock and vibration mounting), linkless 1.06-inch-diameter sway bar, gas struts
Rear ....Trailing beam axle (two leading arms and one track bar locate axle) and coil springs, gas shocks, tubular 1.13-inch-diameter sway bar enclosed in axle beam; high-rate bushings utilized throughout front and rear suspensions
Steering Box Ratio/Type ....14:1/ power rack-and-pinion
Wheels.....................................15x6-inch cast aluminum, four lug
Tires...Goodyear P195/60R-15 Eagle GT

GENERAL:
Curb Weight...............................2700 pounds
Weight Distribution....................61/39 (front/rear)
Fuel Economy (observed)........25 city/35 highway
Quarter-mile...............................*16.45/ 81.04 mph
Skidpad (G)................................0.81

NOTES:
Our Daytona Turbo Z came with optional leather interior, cruise control, full power, premium stereo, and "ground effects" front and rocker panel skirt.

*It should be noted that this run was made at Los Angeles County Drag Strip, located 2700 feet above sea level. The Daytona and SVO do not have identical wastegates; the SVO will maintain its manifold pressure electronically, giving it a significant edge. The Daytona, utilizing a "gauge" or *ambient* referenced wastegate, will only maintain a prescribed differential pressure, and thus suffers at altitude to a slight degree. The NHRA uses a correction factor for altitudes, and for supercharged cars this factor is divided by two. Using the factor, the corrected e.t. and speed would be 16.18 sec. @ 82.41mph.

Four-footed Mustang

The latest in a long line of concept cars to emerge from Ford's Ghia studio in Italy is a high-performance Mustang fitted with an English four-wheel-drive system.

FORD'S STYLISTS at the Ghia studio in Turin have a fine reputation for creating advanced design ideas while still retaining a certain degree of practicality.

The latest embodies those principles but it required the co-operation of a team of Coventry experts to install a permanently-engaged four-wheel-drive system.

The Ghia Vignale Ford Mustang is a high-performance sports coupé with an aerodynamic body and a Ferguson Formula 4WD conversion installed by FF Developments, of Coventry.

The Ghia studio designed and constructed the concept car using a Special Vehicle Operations Mustang underbody.

It is a three-door, four-seat car with flush glass, a smoothly-contoured windscreen with single wiper, low-profile aerodynamic headlamps and a partial belly pan.

Incorporated in the drive line is a transfer box which splits the drive between front and rear wheels and a front propshaft which carries the drive forward from the transfer box to the front axle. Other modifications were made to the front suspension and steering. A viscous-coupling in the transfer box provides automatic limited slip on the central third differential to provide optimum traction under all road and off-road conditions without

the need for a manual lock-out.

The Vignale Mustang is powered by a 1984 Ford SVO four-cylinder 2.3-litre OHC engine, turbocharged with an intercooler. The car is 15ft long, 5ft 8in wide, 4ft 5½in high and has a wheelbase of 8ft 4in.

There is a large glass area to aid all-round visibility and the fixed side windows incorporate sliding sections that can be lowered electrically for paying road tolls or parking fees. Inside, it has digital instrumentation as well as parking and ice sensors. It has 16in cast wheels, tool and first-aid storage compartments on the inside of the quarter panels and individually

folding rear seats.

The radiator air intake is below the aerodynamic front bumper while the handbrake has been integrated into the transmission tunnel console.

Filippo Sapino, Managing Director of Ghia Operations, said: "The Ghia Vignale Mustang has been planned as a concept and is not currently planned for production. However, all Ford concept vehicles incorporate design features that could well find practical application in future Ford products."

Ford's Ghia Vignale Mustang concept car has Ferguson Formula four-wheel-drive

PHOTOGRAPHY DICK KELLEY

Ford Mustang GT

At the zenith of zoom.

• These are good times for the nation. In-flation is down, the price of gas is holding, and the economy is roaring. Oh, sure, we're still far from licking all our troubles, but the state of the Union is unquestionably positive. And, as always when America feels good, we're ready to get high on horsepower.

If ever there was a car poised to take advantage of current events, it's the new Mustang GT. We don't use the term "new" loosely, either. Though the basic design is six model years old—*very* old in people years—it's been thoroughly rejuvenated by the Ford engineering department for 1985. The power curve now bulges bigger than ever, there are significant chassis improvements, and there's more speed under-foot than ever before—and last year's Mustang GT was no tortoise.

Why has all this attention been lavished on a car clearly in its sunset years? "It's the ethic of continuous improvement," says Ford president Donald Petersen, proudly referring to his master plan to keep upgrading all model lines throughout their lifetimes. Then there's the age-old rivalry with Chevrolet. Camaro development is anything but stagnant these days.

The impressive thing about all this is just how thorough the make-over is. Ford didn't just do the easy stuff. About the only visual refinements are a new nosepiece and some different body-side moldings.

Most of the improvements are out of sight. The body structure, for instance, was stiffened by using structural adhesives at all major sheetmetal joints in addition to the standard pinch welds. Dash-to-cowl side reinforcements were added as well.

The drivetrain got a full going-over. The GT's 4.9-liter V-8 was treated to a roller

cam to reduce internal friction. The cam is also a hotter grind than was used last year, for more power. A set of tubular headers improves exhaust scavenging, and all-new exhaust plumbing reduces back pressure by 40 percent. A two-speed accessory drive spins the air conditioner, the alternator, the water pump, and the power-steering pump at half speed above idle, contributing 5 hp. In all, the revisions add up to 35 hp, bringing the total power output to a whopping 210 hp at 4600 rpm. (The only other change in the engine bay is the deletion of the 2.3-liter turbocharged four-cylinder from the GT.)

The five-speed gearbox has also come in for an overhaul. The first, third, and fifth gear throws, each of which used to be a stretch, have been shortened by 27 percent. Internally, the gear ratios have been juggled for more dig off the line.

Vehicle type: front-engine, rear-wheel-drive, 4-passenger, 3-door sedan

Estimated base price: $10,500

Engine type: V-8, iron block and heads, 1x4-bbl carburetor	
Displacement	302 cu in, 4942cc
Power (SAE net)	210 bhp @ 4600 rpm
Transmission	5-speed
Wheelbase	100.5 in
Length	179.3 in
Curb weight	3000 lbs
EPA fuel economy, city driving (projected)	17 mpg

Every bit as much effort was put into improving the GT's road manners, which is nothing if not good news. Mustangs have always been front-line power cars; it's their handling that's been gimpy. For 1985, variable-rate springs have been fitted all around, and the gas-filled front struts and rear shocks are valved about 50 percent tighter. The quad-shock rear-suspension layout introduced in the middle of last season for the SVO has been added, and the rear anti-sway bar is larger. Most important, a set of gummy, unidirectional P225/60VR-15 Goodyear Eagle VR60s on new fifteen-by-seven-inch wheels has been stuffed into the wheel wells.

Even the GT's interior has been tuned. Some of the changes—a new dash facing and an SVO-style three-hole steering wheel—were introduced in mid-1984. The GT's door upholstery and Lear Siegler buckets—which are quite comfortable—are new. Our only regret is that Ford can't seem to find the money to replace the Mustang's old-fashioned dashboard.

Everything Ford *has* changed, however, seems to work like a charm—at least as far as we could tell during our short proving-grounds session. The true test, of course, will be out on the road, but that will have to wait until the production cars are ready. For now, we can confirm that this is one strong runner. The nicest thing is that the motor no longer overpowers the tires. It used to be that a heavy right foot at the wrong time would make a Mustang GT drive as if it were on Jell-O. Not anymore. The steering feels connected now and much more reassuring. Indeed, there's a harmony here that we've never before encountered in a Mustang.

Getting back to our original thesis on good times and fast cars in America, we predict that this will be a strong year for the Mustang GT. The timing couldn't be better for a car at the zenith of its zoom.

—*Rich Ceppos*

A great engine gets even better

1985 Ford Mustang GT

by Ron Grable

PHOTOGRAPHY BY BOB D'OLIVO

Since the introduction of the SVO Mustang, hyped as the new-generation or future-direction Mustang, there has been heated speculation concerning the future of the iron V-8 GT. The high-tech SVO has not exactly knocked 'em dead in the showrooms yet, and the GT Mustangs still outsell their sibling by a sizeable margin.

The essence of the SVO is high performance from a small-displacement powerplant that can be fuel efficient *and* performance oriented. And to achieve this, the 2.3-liter SVO must be turned at high engine speeds and use relatively high boost levels; and this is perhaps part of the buyer resistance to the car. (The other part is a $6000 price disparity in favor of the V-8.) To use the SVO in a performance mode, you have to drive it like you're mad at it. When you do, its performance is outstanding but something you cannot take lightly; you have to mentally prepare yourself, and then wring its little neck.

The Ford V-8s, by comparison, have all that wonderful *torque*. You do remember torque, don't you? Think back to the days of loafing along the highway in top gear, with

a big V-8 under your foot. If you needed to pass someone, or climb a steep hill, or even if you felt like slamming your pals back into the seat, you could push down with your right foot and it just happened—right *now*. No need to shift down a couple gears, no need to get the turbo spooled up, no need to worry much about over-revving. It was always right there, with no drama. Those big hugga-mugga motors devoured fuel (who cared, fuel was 30¢ per gallon), but they were easy to drive and you never needed to worry about being in the wrong gear.

Which may go a long way toward explaining the continuing popularity of the Mustang GTs. They still do have the lovely axle-creaking torque reminiscent of another time, and the 1985 offerings from FoMoCo have taken another small step up the ladder by producing even more power/torque. This is a result of a couple old hot-rodding tricks: a higher-performance cam with roller tappets and tubular stainless steel headers. The roller tappets allow faster, earlier valve openings, compared with flat tappets, and enable the engine men to increase the volumetric efficiency (engineerese for better breathing).

Being able to get more air into the engine means provisions have to be made to get it out, and the tubular headers do an admirable job of that. The normal cast iron manifolds are very restrictive due in part to the high pumping losses, nor do they allow for pulse tuning, where the gasses leaving one cylinder are used to help evacuate an adjacent one. Individual tubular headers do.

With all this not-so-subtle hot-rodding, Ford was able to get 210 hp at 4600 rpm (a gain of 34 hp) and 265 lb-ft of torque at 3400 rpm (up 20 lb-ft) from the '85 5.0-liter engine. The engine compartment has always been the strong suit for the Mustang line, but the '85 is even more wonderful. The increased torque is very noticeable and the engine revs almost like a race motor: quick, with a throaty growl that resonates right at peak power. In 1st and 2nd gears, it's all too easy to climb past redline since the engine is accelerating so hard. Close your eyes and roll the windows down and you'd swear you were in a 289 Cobra.

With all the available torque, wheelspin is a serious problem in quarter-mile acceleration testing.

Most techniques send the rear tires up in smoke, but after many tries, we settled on a lurch-it-outta-the-hole/throttle-down procedure. Even then, if the throttle was too early, excessive wheelspin was the unwanted result. Some of the Ford engineers claim to have recorded sub-7-sec 0-60-mph times. We were unable to duplicate that on this day for a couple reasons—high ambient temperatures and less than optimum surface—but our best 0-60 time of 7.08 sec indicates the possibility of an optimized time in the "sixes." Heady stuff indeed for a 3013-lb smog-legal production car.

Some engineering effort has been expended on the manual 5-speed, with the specific goal of reducing shifting effort and lever travel. Leverages have been changed and friction reduced to achieve the desired result, and the Mustang shift linkage is one of the best we've used, hooked to a "big" V-8. The rear axle ratios have been changed in the '85 Mustang GT and reduced numerically to 2.73:1 without—or 3.08:1 with—the limited slip differential.

To help get this increased power to the ground, a new 15 x 7-in. cast aluminum wheel is standard equipment, along with the new 225/60VR15 Goodyear unidirectional "gatorback" tires. The virtues of this tire are well documented by now, and they contribute significantly to the Mustang GT handling equation, offering good cornering power, wet traction, and high predictability.

Borrowing a page from the SVO styling book, a revised SVOesque grille and integrated front air dam are new exterior items for 1985 on the GT. Integral fog lamps are included in the front spoiler, and the whole front-end treatment works well, with a coordinated aero-functional look. Most exterior trim and body accents have been changed from the '84 gloss black to a more subdued charcoal. Interior changes are minimal with some updating on previously optional equipment items, such as articulated sports seats, which are now standard equipment in the GT.

With the increased performance of the '85 GT Mustang, we are anxiously anticipating our first chance to do a full road test. In the past the chassis has been the weak link in the Mustang performance chain, but during a quick skidpad run at FoMoCo's proving grounds, we were impressed by the balance of the GT. It definitely seemed better than previous versions we've tested, so maybe—just maybe—the engineers haven't told us everything.

Let's see now, the IROC Camaro is touting more horsepower this year, the Dodge Daytona Turbo Z has its trick new transient boost system. Could a showdown be in order? Chevy versus Ford versus Chrysler. Sounds like an advertisement for a late '60s Trans-Am race, doesn't it? Sounds like fun, as a matter of fact. (MT)

DATA

Ford Mustang GT

POWERTRAIN

Vehicle configuration	Front engine, rear drive
Engine configuration	V-8, OHV
Displacement	4950 cc (302 cu in.)
Max. power (SAE net)	210 hp @ 4600 rpm
Max torque (SAE net)	265 lb-ft @ 3400 rpm
Transmission	5-sp. man.
Final drive	2.73:1

CHASSIS

Suspension, f/r	Independent/live axle
Brakes, f/r	Disc/disc
Steering	Rack and pinion
Wheels	15 x 7.0-in. alloy
Tires	P225/60VR15

DIMENSIONS

Wheelbase	2550 mm (100.5 in.)
Overall length	4549 mm (179.1 in.)
Curb weight	1362 kg (3013 lb)
Fuel capacity	58.3 L (15.4 gal)

PERFORMANCE

0-60 mph	7.08 sec
Standing quarter mile	15.51 sec/89.7 mph
Braking, 60-0	164 ft
Skidpad	0.84 g

With an unchanged interior and only minor molding and front bumper revisions outside, the big news for the '85 Mustang GT is under the hood. Roller tappets, stainless steel exhaust headers, and a revised camshaft now squeeze 210 hp out of the 5.0-liter V-8. Shiftless drivers be warned: This kind of power isn't available with an automatic.

Get it together–Buckle up.

The Ford Mustang GT.

This is one powerfully built machine. On demand, a 5.0 liter High Output V-8 engine delivers 210 horsepower.* No brag. Just fact.

Turnstyle: Equal parts of power and control.

Mustang GT's got what it takes to control the balance of power. Quick ratio rack and pinion steering for handling precision. Gas-filled shocks and struts on a Quadra-Shock performance suspension. Variable rate springs. Stiffer bushings and anti-sway bars for added stability in the straights, confidence in the curves. And on 15x7 alloy wheels, P225/60VR15 Goodyear Gatorback. The same tires that broke the .95-g barrier in skidpad tests.

Internal control.

When a performance car changes directions, the car should move, not the driver. That's why Mustang GT comes equipped with articulated driving seats. They adjust to fit a wide variety of bodystyles comfortably, securely. And for your information, they face an instrument panel whose analog gauges measure how much, how many, how fast.

Best-Built American Cars.

"Quality is Job 1." A 1984 survey established that Ford makes the best-built American cars. This is based on an average of problems reported by owners in the prior six months on 1981-1983 models designed and built in the U.S.

Lifetime Service Guarantee.

See your participating Ford Dealer for details.

When it comes to performance, Mustang GT does it right. And left.

We've had our fun. Now it's your turn.

*Based on SAE standard J-1349.

Have you driven a Ford... lately?

CAMARO IROC-Z

The further fisticuffs of America's favorite musclecars

MAYBE WE SHOULD have done it at Caesars Palace in Las Vegas. Booked the sports arena. Sold tickets. Taken bets. Sat back and listened to the announcer's familiar bawl: "In this corner, weighing 3425 lb and wearing black sheet metal, Ford Mustang GT. In the opposite corner, weighing 3440 lb, wearing yellow sheet metal, Chevrolet Camaro IROC-Z." Some words about the rules, a handshake and the match would be on. A rematch, in a way, because the two adversaries had met before. Not in the ring, of course, but on the track at Willow Springs International Raceway in Rosamond, California in August of this year. The occasion, R&T's comparison test of eight Showroom Stock GTs, a fight that neither the 1984 Camaro Z28 nor the 1985 Mustang GT prototype won. That honor went to the 1984 Corvette. But hold that count for a second. The Vette and the Nissan 300ZX, runner-up in that match, are GTs costing a heck of a lot more than the Ford and the Chevy. Yet, in

our comparison the Mustang and Camaro were (as we say in th fight game) con-ten-duhs. The 1985 GT and IROC-Z are ve sions of models we would have described five years ago a musclecars, brute force straight-line automobiles with very littl finesse or overall balance in the other areas we find importan handling, ride, braking, steering, etc. In recent years thes streetwise kids (does Woodward Ave ring a bell?) have learne to do more than just punch. They move, which in automotiv jargon translates into corner, steer and stop. And pound fo pound, inch for inch, they are real affordable contenders in th heavyweight sports coupe division.

At the time of our August test we weren't able to match th Mustang GT against the 1985 IROC-Z because that car was (s to speak) still in training. So we waited until Chevy said "Now! and staged a rematch. Not at Caesars or the Garden, but at Wa terford Hills, a 1.5-mile road course located about 26 mile

Larry Fletcher,
project engineer,
Chevrolet Camaro
IROC-Z.

COMPARISON
R&T
ROAD TEST

FORD
vs
MUSTANG GT

PHOTOS BY JOE RUSZ

northeast of Detroit. Maybe the Mustang and Camaro project engineers wanted to put on gloves and duke it out in the ring. But we preferred to don driving suits and helmets and do our fighting on the track, against the clock. At the wheel of Ford's and Chevrolet's latest.

Mustang GT

IN THE fight game they'd call this one Rocky. Not just because, like the boxer in the film, the Ford was trying to make a comeback of sorts. But because this is a bruiser of a car with 210 bhp and 265 lb-ft of tire-boiling torque. A musclecar with the emphasis on muscle—from its 5.0-liter high output V-8 with roller-tappet, long-duration, high-lift camshaft, to its progressive-rate springs with dual Koni rear shocks. A hefty 5-speed close-ratio gearbox and extra-wide alloy wheels with swarthy 225/60VR-15 Goodyear gatorback tires are all designed to help

the Mustang GT play rough. Like Rocky.

By the way, this jet-black GT should look familiar. It's the same car that we used in our SSGT comparison test and the only 1985 Mustang GT in existence (because production of the 1985s had not yet begun) at the time of this test.

Camaro IROC-Z

DUB IT The Kid. More than just tough, it's wiry. With 190 horsepower it can deliver quite a punch. But the Chevy's strong point is footwork as typified by its well balanced, almost neutral feel. More about that later. First, some vital statistics about this new contender.

The IROC-Z is the latest derivation of Chevrolet's popular F-body and represents a further extension of the Z28 concept. Named after the Camaro-body racing cars used in the International Race of Champions, the IROC-Z looks a bit different ➤

*Jim Kennedy,
project engineer,
Ford Mustang GT.*

47

than the Z28 that is still being sold, albeit without the latest goodies. Anyway, the IROC-Z has fog lamps set in their own distinctive grille, body-color rocker panels, IROC decals affixed to the doors and aluminum wheels that are not only visually but dimensionally distinctive. They are an inch larger in diameter and width than the Z28 wheels (16 x 8 vs 15 x 7 in.) and are shod with P245/50VR-16 Goodyear gatorbacks rather than the garden variety P215/60R-15 Eagle GTs used by the Z28. Because of their increased width, the new rims' offset is different too. It has been moved inward to allow the whole meaty package to fit inside the wheel wells.

The change in tires alone contributes substantially to the IROC-Z's improved handling, which is further enhanced by revalved (stiffer) front shocks, Bilstein gas-over rear shocks and a 1-mm larger diameter rear anti-roll bar. One more thing—Chevy says the whole car sits about 15 mm lower than the Z28. This is achieved by using (in the factory's words) "one code lower" springs. In other words, the assembly workers go through a stockpile of Z28 coils and pick out all the shorties for the IROC-Z.

Other changes, though more subtle, are nonetheless important and include power assisted steering with higher effort valving, increased front-end caster for better on-center feel and frame-rail bracing to minimize front-end chassis flex and thus decrease compliance steer.

There's one more feature that sets the IROC-Z apart from lesser Camaros, the new for 1985, 215-bhp V-8 with Tuned Port Injection. Unfortunately, this powerplant is not available with a manual transmission at this time. And because we were once again evaluating these cars with an eye toward SSGT competition where a standard transmission is mandatory, in our track test we were forced to use Chevy's only high output engine equipped with a 5-speed, the so-called L69. This 5.0-liter, 4-barrel equipped V-8 has the same horsepower (190 bhp) and torque (240 lb-ft) as last year's powerplant. However, with the expectation that sometime during 1985 Chevy will mate the hot 5.0 liter with a 5-speed manual gearbox, we also measured the acceleration of an automatic TPI IROC-Z.

The Arena

THAT WE needed a road course for our test was a foregone conclusion. That we chose Waterford Hills can be explained in two words: convenience and neutrality. Because the cars were prototypes that were based at each company's proving grounds near Detroit, we decided it would be easier to bring the mountain to Mohammed, so to speak. After all, we wanted to have the respective project engineers present but realized that because of their busy schedules it would be inconvenient to drag them too far from their factories. We also didn't want to be accused of giving either team a home-court advantage: i.e., testing both cars on a proving ground road course familiar only to one of the two. So rather than send a dozen people on a cross-country trek to a distant circuit such as Mid-Ohio, we opted for Waterford Hills, a pocket-size plant that is less than an hour's drive from Ford and Chevrolet. As tidy as this circuit is, the track has one major failing: It's too short for fast cars such as the Mustang and the Camaro. Neither got a chance to unwind in 4th gear (5th is generally too tall for even longer courses such as Mid-Ohio), although both GT and IROC-Z were able to demonstrate their dazzling acceleration, impressive braking and of course their commendable handling.

Sparring

BEFORE CLIMBING into the ring for the big fight, we thought it would be a good idea to watch the challengers work out—on the dragstrip and on the skidpad. Ford graciously let us use the north-south straightaway and the skidpad at its Dearborn pro ing grounds and on the day before our track test, Assistant Eng neering Editor Kim Reynolds instrumented the Mustang an Camaro and measured each car's straight-line and lateral acce eration, braking distances and slalom times. And just to see ho much difference 25 bhp can make, Kim also measured the acce eration of the TPI-equipped, automatic-transmission IROC-Z.

When it comes to acceleration, the muscular Mustang has t edge over the standard-shift IROC-Z. The GT goes from 0 to 6 mph in 7.2 seconds and reaches the quarter mile in 15.9 se The same trip in the IROC-Z takes 8.1 and 16.5 sec respe tively. But ponder the potential of the IROC-Z automatic who 7.3 sec 0 to 60 and 15.8 sec quarter-mile times were almo identical to the Ford's. Can you imagine what a standard tran mission will do for the Chevy when a 5-speed is finally coupl to the 215-bhp engine?

Getting there (0 to 60, the quarter mile) may be half the fu but stopping is another matter. From 60 mph, the Ford stops 151 ft vs the Chevy's 160. However, the tables are turned fro 80 to zero mph as the Camaro's 267 ft beats the Mustang's sto ping distance by 4 ft. Short distances and virtually a draw fro either speed. The Z is helped by wide rims and tires that produ a larger footprint than the GT's, but its slightly mushy pedal an unresponsive feel make modulation more difficult. The GT, contrast, exhibits better feel, though still a less than optim relationship between pedal pressure and retardation force.

The Chevy's wide footprint also helps the car's lateral acce eration, 0.845g compared with the Ford's 0.792g. But in t slalom the Mustang has the advantage and averages 60.9 vs 59 mph through the cones. The reason is simple: The GT has mo understeer and understeering cars are more manueverab around the pylons than oversteerers.

The Bout

NO FLYING fists, no thuds or grunts signifying a well plac body blow. Just a lot of tire squealing, a sound synon mous with showroom stock racing. In the modern-day high pe formance production car, screaming tires drown out even t exhaust note, which is fairly audible given the nature of the cars' low back-pressure exhaust systems. The plan at Waterfo Hills was to let each driver take a few laps in one car, then h into the other, comparing performance, handling, braking an such, and chipping away at lap times. The trio of testers al noted each car's other strengths and weaknesses before sittil down to choose a winner.

At the bell it was the Ford, punching its way to a clear-c victory in acceleration and straight-line speed. At Waterfo Hills the black bomber blasted from corner to corner with ligh ning-like quickness. The GT's wallop comes from its braw V-8, which revs freely to its 5900-rpm redline where it begins sound a bit rough. But there's no need to twist the engine's ta when there's torque aplenty, enough to spin the wheels in pra tically any gear. And induce oversteer, which may be what Fo had in mind after all. You see, the Mustang is an inhere understeerer and by using the throttle to induce oversteer ye can set the car and get it to transition nicely through the turr At Waterford Hills we found that one could turn respectable l times using only 3rd gear, thanks to the broad torque curve.

The powerplant's shortcomings are minor—a stumble in le hand turns where the carburetor float interferes with fuel flow one of the jets; and the on-off cycling of the Two-Spe Accesory Drive (TSAD). It cuts in at 3100 rpm to reduce (half-speed) the rotational speed of the alternator, water pum power steering pump and air conditioning compressor. Ford e gineers say this is primarily to improve fuel economy althou they admit the system also reduces horsepower drag by 15 bh

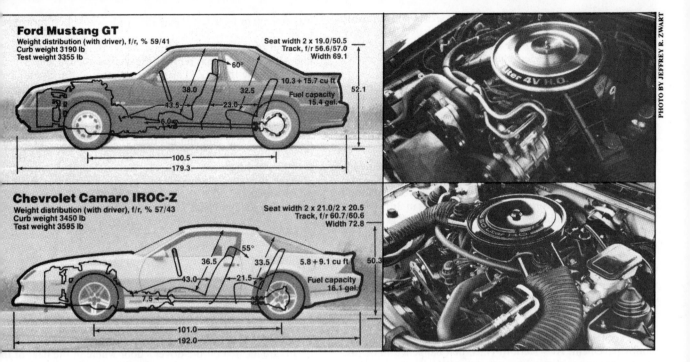

Ford Mustang GT
Weight distribution (with driver), f/r, % 59/41
Curb weight 3190 lb
Test weight 3355 lb
Seat width 2 x 19.0/50.5
Track, f/r 56.6/57.0
Width 69.1

Chevrolet Camaro IROC-Z
Weight distribution (with driver), f/r, % 57/43
Curb weight 3450 lb
Test weight 3595 lb
Seat width 2 x 21.0/2 x 20.5
Track, f/r 60.7/60.6
Width 72.8

PHOTO BY JEFFREY R. ZWART

GENERAL DATA

	Chevrolet Camaro IROC-Z	Ford Mustang GT
Base price	est $11,700	$9885
Price as tested¹	est $14,380	$10,974
Layout	front engine/rwd	front engine/rwd
Engine type	ohv V-8	ohv V-8
Bore x stroke, mm	94.9 x 88.4	101.6 x 76.2
Displacement, cc	5001	4942
Compression ratio	9.5:1	8.3:1
Bhp @ rpm, SAE net	190 @ 4800	210 @ 4600
Torque @ rpm, lb-ft	240 @ 3200	265 @ 3400
Carburetion	one Rochester (4V)	one Holley (4V)
Transmission	5-sp manual	5-sp manual
Gear ratios, :1	2.95/1.94/	3.35/1.93/
	1.34/1.00/0.63	1.29/1.00/0.68
Final drive ratio, :1	3.73	3.08
Steering type	rack & pinion, power assisted	rack & pinion, power assisted
Brake system, f/r	10.5-in. vented discs/ 10.5-in. vented discs	10.1-in. vented discs/ 9.0 x 1.8-in. drums
Wheels	cast alloy, 16 x 8	cast alloy, 15 x 7
Tires	Goodyear Eagle VR50, P245/50VR-16	Goodyear Eagle VR60, P225/60VR-15
Suspension, f/r	modified MacPherson struts, lower A-arms, coil springs, tube shocks, anti-roll bar/live axle on trailing arms, torque arm & Panhard rod; coil springs, tube shocks, anti-roll bar	modified MacPherson struts, lower A-arms, separate coil springs and Koni adj tube shocks, anti-roll bar/live axle on angled upper & lower trailing arms, coil springs, dual tube shocks, anti-roll bar

Price as tested includes: For the Chevrolet Camaro, air cond, AM/FM stereo/cassette, elect. window lifts, interior group, cruise control, misc options (est $2680); for the Ford Mustang, air cond ($743), elect. window lifts ($198), AM/FM stereo/cassette ($148)

PERFORMANCE

	Chevrolet Camaro IROC-Z	Ford Mustang GT
Acceleration:		
Time to distance, sec:		
0–100 ft	3.5	3.2
0–500 ft	9.5	9.0
0–1320 ft (¼ mi)	16.5	15.9
Speed at end of ¼ mi, mph	90.0	91.0
Time to speed, sec:		
0–30 mph	3.2	2.7
0–60 mph	8.1	7.2
0–80 mph	13.4	12.3
0–100 mph	20.9	19.1
Top speed, mph	est 135	est 135
Fuel economy, mpg	est 16.0	est 15.5
Brakes:		
Stopping distance, ft, from:		
60 mph	160	151
80 mph	267	271
Pedal effort for 0.5g stop, lb	22	35
Fade, % increase in effort, 6 stops from 60 mph @ 0.5g	20	nil
Overall brake rating	very good	very good
Handling:		
Lateral acceleration, g	0.845	0.792
Slalom speed, mph	59.7	60.9
Interior noise, dBA:		
Idle in neutral	61	54
Maximum 1st gear	83	81
Constant 30 mph	72	65
50 mph	73	69
70 mph	76	76
90 mph	79	78

CALCULATED DATA

	Chevrolet Camaro IROC-Z	Ford Mustang GT
Lb/bhp (test weight)	18.9	16.0
Mph/1000 rpm (5th gear)	31.5	34.7
Engine revs/mi (60 mph)	1905	1730
Piston travel, ft/mi	1105	865
R&T steering index	0.92	0.92
Brake swept area, sq in./ton	171	164

But we say the surging that occurs when it kicks in and out loads and unloads the engine, hindering performance. An aside: Early 1985 Mustang GTs won't have TSAD because Ford was able to meet its 21-mpg gas-guzzler requirement without it. But expect the system later in the production year or in 1986.

By comparison, the IROC-Z's engine seems tame—in the literal sense of the word. Although it doesn't have the gut-wrenching torque of the Mustang GT, it does quite well with what it has (240 lb-ft isn't exactly chopped liver, you know). You can induce power oversteer with the L69, but when you attempt to, it's more like turning a rheostat than like throwing a switch. The Chevy V-8 is also quite flexible and will rev to the redline although, unlike the Ford, it gets winded near the end. On the road course, one of our drivers found that he preferred shifting down to 2nd gear for corners rather than staying in 3rd. The car felt more nimble to him, probably because this lower gear's multiplication, whether on or off throttle, translated into a more responsive helm and a car that was easier to point.

Round two: braking. Although the two cars seemed more or less equal in straight-line stopping, out on the racetrack it wasn't much of a contest. Even though the Ford has rear drums, its quad rear shocks cinch the axle down ensuring stable reaction to heavy braking. The Chevy, on the other hand, is not sufficiently damped and the car develops severe axle tramp when the otherwise excellent 4-wheel disc brakes are applied strongly on bumpy pavement. At Waterford Hills, that happened to be just when approaching the first turn, and this behavior made it difficult to make a smooth transition into the corner. 'Twas somewhat unnerving too!

The IROC-Z rallied in the handling round. The Chevy's balanced handling paid off on the road course. Once again, those big wheels and tires just stick. What's more, optimal matching of shocks, springs and anti-roll bars give the Camaro an almost neutral feel. Mild oversteer can be induced by lifting off the throttle, and the rear end can be positioned with judicious application of the same. The IROC-Z, in fact, is an easy car to drive fast and at the end of our test session we were not surprised to find that with a best time of 1 minute 26.70 seconds, the Chevy

Chevrolet Camaro IROC-Z.

was more than 1-sec faster than the Ford—whose best turned out to be 1:27.78.

About the Mustang's handling: We'd call it fun but challenging. Although Ford has retuned the chassis, the GT understeers more than the IROC-Z. This is due, in part, to wheels and tires that are an inch narrower than the Camaro's. The GT's suspension is on the stiff side and this makes the car feel more like a pure race car (albeit one with street radials, rather than racing tires). Yes, it's fun to fling the Ford into a corner, hang out the tail, light the rear tires and flat-track it. Spectacular! But it's not the fast way, as our trio of testers found out.

In the fight to the finish, the Camaro landed some solid punches in styling and in ease of operation (shifting, pedal action). About the IROC-Z's looks: clean with attention to aerodynamics; good integration of spoilers and side skirts. True, the GT takes a few swings in the same direction—there's a new SVO Mustang nose plus fender flares and a rear spoiler. But the Ford can't match the Chevy's swoopiness and, we suspect, its C_x. About the Camaro's controls: Shifting and clutch efforts are lower and the steering feels less twitchy than in the Mustang, although the Ford's steering sensitivity lessens at speed. Earlier we mentioned that Chevrolet had increased front caster and this is borne out by the excellent on-center feel of the steering. The IROC-Z's interior design is cleaner and the electric window-lift switches are out of the way, on the console. The GT's, you may recall, are located on the driver's door where in the heat of the moment, they are easily triggered by a left knee looking for support in right turns. Ouch!

The Decision?

THIS IS a case of you pick 'em. The Mustang won the acceleration round and had an edge in braking. But the Camaro slugged its way to the top in the other rounds (handling, balance, looks).

Both champions put up a great battle and we're not sure we could pick an absolute winner. On a short course where handling is important, the title would go the the IROC-Z. On a long course where horsepower and high speed count, the crown would

Chevrolet Camaro IROC-Z.

Ford Mustang GT.

probably go to the Mustang GT. And on the road we'd be in for another standoff because both cars score so well in our fun-to-drive category. For example, with horsepower and torque to spare, the Mustang doesn't even draw a sharp breath when tooling around town. Its power assisted steering makes the car quite manueverable in spite of its relatively large size.

The L69-equipped Camaro may have less horsepower than the Mustang but this doesn't impair its driveability on the road. The engine can be lugged without undue protest and still pull smartly up to the redline.

GT and IROC-Z are comfortable with great seats and appreciated options such as effective air conditioning and excellent

AM/FM stereo/cassette radios. The two cars even ride reasonably well—as smoothly as can be expected from coupes with such high levels of handling. The duo's looks are distinctive: The Ford's are beefy and what some would call macho; the Chevy's are lean and athletic. To sum up the two cars' natures, we could say that the Ford represents a modern-day musclecar while the Chevy is a poor man's Corvette.

Another rematch? Perhaps, when the 1986 IROC-Z with the TPI engine and 5-speed finishes its training. Of course, Ford won't allow the Mustang GT to get out of shape and this means we'll be in for another close fight. Maybe we could stage it in the Astrodome.

Ford Mustang GT.

HIT OR MYTH?

In America, Ford's Mustang sports car is a machine of macho legend. But how does the latest V8 ragtop stand up to a wintry Britain?

STORY BY RUSSELL BULGIN
PHOTOGRAPHY BY MAURICE ROWE

Americans grew up in the convertible. Some were born in them, and many, many more were conceived in them. Too many others died in them — from the wild kid down the block whom everybody in the neighbourhood liked, to a president the whole world liked. It's too much to expect that if we bring the car type back, we can bring the people like them back. Let it, and them, slip further and further back in memory where every afternoon is sun filled, every girl pretty, every gas tank full, and every top waterproof. It's the best country in which to drive an open car. We're only sorry that our children can't visit it, and will have to be content to live it all secondhand.
WARREN WEITH: **The Last American Convertibles**

It was the first of the long-term plans to put something together for the kids. The components were in the system; all we had to do was put a youth wrapper around it.
LEE IACOCCA: **ex-General Manager of Ford and driving force behind Mustang**

WRONG, WARREN, wrong. Long before the rise of the Nike running shoe as a status symbol or celebrity aerobics as the new narcissism, Americans worshipped fresh air. More than a simple health benefit, it stands as a metaphor for the great outdoors, a lifestyle that is a sepia-toned alternative to the downtown hustle. So the convertible was never going to die out: it might wane, but given the cyclical nature of whim and fashion, it would return as yet another profit centre in the auto dealership of life.

So now you can purchase almost any "specialty car" on the American market complete with a ragtop produced by the factory or a host of aftermarket tin-snippers. You can gross-out over a shortened, convertible Cadillac Seville, or have the roof sliced off a Toyota Celica Supra in any number of locations stateside.

But the Mustang, of course, is the perfect candidate for getting soft in the headlining. It's not so much a car as a legendary image. A shape which was a Hollywood starlet on wheels. Revealed in 1964 as a slim, crisp, elegant newcomer brimming with sass and verve, it gradually got lost in a morass of middle-aged spread and failed facelifts. Every year it got soggier, softer, and somehow more confused — more fake wood added to chrome dash-panel appliqués. Then came the Mustang II, a horribly malformed bastard offspring, a car where every single bodyline

as wrong. It presented a sitting target to the Japanese invaders. Ford's third Mustang was revealed in 1979 as an American response to the Orient, the energy crisis, and trying to re-establish the Mustang name. It continues today.

And a convertible Mustang is the perfect car for America 1984. Fuel prices are down, so a 5.0-litre V8 engine makes as much sense as it ever will. The name itself is a blast from the past and a convertible sums up all the images that Ronald Reagan pandered to in his election campaign. A simpler America, before Vietnam, recreational drugs or OPEC, the downhome values captured in a Norman Rockwell painting: instant nostalgia.

The Ford Mustang GT 5.0 convertible *Motor* drove was reputedly the personal wheels of a high-ranking Ford executive, a choice of car which must reflect on the hidden strain of tap-dancing through the corridors of power. It was big, white and bland, with a dirty matt-black stripe slurping over the bonnet.

In its styling, it approached mid-life crisis, not knowing whether to wig out and toughen up, or become restrained and discreet. The blacked-out bonnet shouted youth, the awkward white remainder suggested torpor. Only in the droop-nose and biplane-winged SVO guise does the Mustang remotely resemble 1984: in less calculated models, the Mustang is a slightly awkward amalgam of American and European influences whipped up into a nondescript coupé.

Inside, the grey trim is neat, the instrument panel basically unchanged since 1979 save for the adoption of mock Allen-screws dotted over the facia. Perhaps that is to fool the driver into thinking he is controlling either something very high-tech or an F-16 jet fighter: more likely the concept is ripped off, lock, stock and

injection moulding, from the Chevrolet Camaro which sports a similarly lame-brain decor. Just so the soft top has all the comforts of home, the Mustang is fitted with a comprehensive air conditioning system for those days when either the weather or the neighbourhood you're driving through gets a little hard to relate to.

To start the engine, press the clutch and then turn the key. When you come to pocket the ignition key a little button beneath the column must be pressed before it can be wriggled free: nothing is simple. The seat belts fall off your shoulder unless you put them on with a door open. At idle the engine sends out a subdued V8 woofle, a distant rumble as the idle speed paces back and forth. It is a powerful sound, as American as a Chuck Berry guitar break. And just about as old.

Performance, too, is pretty good: a Sierra XR4i would have a distinct edge but there is enough urge to send the Mustang sailing into corners quick enough for the Novocaine steering to set the pulse throbbing in time with the engine. For while the chassis is pretty competent, if you can handle stabs of power oversteer when things get tough, the steering is as horrible as Bruce Springsteen's dress-sense. It is low geared, feel-less and power-assisted to a degree sufficient to hold the car on opposite lock. Worse than all that, it is numb: you are never quite sure what the car will do. Which is a pity as roll is minimal, and the actual balance of the car, if oversteery, is reasonably predictable and safe.

A five-speed gearbox is a surprise, but top is a super-tall sop to Sheikh Yamani. This car pulls just 1500 rpm at the US legal maximum of 55 mph: pressing the throttle in fifth simply brings on an increase in under-bonnet volume. The speedometer dial stops at 85 mph after a 270° arc — but the needle keeps on travelling. Maximum speed of the Mustang is thus "Y": that being the last letter of the "Unleaded Gasoline Only" reminder embossed on the speedo, and the one place where you can peg the needle flat-out. Change quality is good, with a long, deliberate movement through the box: fast changes are neither needed nor encouraged.

Sometimes the ride feels a little restless: occasionally the rear-view mirror moves laterally. Torsional stiffness is not a Mustang strongpoint. Drive slowly along a bumpy track and you can feel the front and rear ends of the car shuffling asynchronously. Ease a wheel over the kerb and the car suffers midriff sag. Inside, the hood mechanism is exposed as a black skeleton crawling up the rear pillars, but the power-operated top — with glass rear pane — snuggles itself down quickly and tidily, though it looks less stylish.

Nor does it leak, but there is a vacuum-cleaner roar from where the electrically-operated rear quarter windows butt against the hood which, at 70 mph, is insistent enough — especially when combined with a bass-heavy radio that makes reggae sound like bluegrass — to leave you hearing only in mono.

But the Mustang is now a period piece — it's just unfortunate that 1979 wasn't a great period for American cars. In its engine, soft-top, feather-touch steering and tyre-smoking wet road traction, the Mustang belongs to another age. Just like Ronald Reagan, it seems pretty docile until you push it too hard, whereupon it just curls up and purrs. If it explains anything clearly, it is the rise of Japanese cars in what were wholly American sectors of the market: compared to a Mustang, the Toyota Celica Supra feels like a Ferrari Daytona. But Ford have got that angle taped as well: the next Mustang is reputed to have been developed hand in hand with Mazda . . .

Ford Mustang GT

Time to catch the 302, and we're not talking Amtrak.

• In the course of its rather assertive advertising, BMW shows us the tail end of a 533i and promises "a decompression chamber for the highly motivated."

Maybe. But wouldn't you rather have a V-8, particularly if that V-8 has the refinement we've always associated with the Germans' fours and sixes, and the go power the Germans can only dream of in their exports to America?

It's easy to get the wrong idea about the Mustang GT. You can thumb back to this road test's spec page, glom onto the 6.4-second 0-to-60 time, and conclude we've finally found the pavement burner of our adolescent fantasies.

Wrong. This is a car for adults. It's okay if you're highly motivated. It's okay if you can afford a whole lot more than the test car's $9885 base price. It's even okay if you're currently driving a German decompression chamber. In fact, it's probably better if you are, because then you'll be in a position to appreciate how close this Mustang GT comes to the German definition of a serious car.

A serious car starts with a look, and Ford, maybe because it has more international

blood pumping through its engineering veins than any other Detroit automaker, seems to understand the difference between what is German and what is Atari. If you're not careful with the options sheet, the inside of your Camaro or Firebird will look like Tokyo by night, but the Mustang GT has real gauges with black faces and white markings. The outside is restrained as well. Apart from the blackout hood treatment, "GT" is the only proclamation you'll find anywhere, unless you count the 60-series gatorback Goodyears that fill the fender openings. And even they say "German": they're moderate in their profile, which is the German way. Detroit, in contrast, tends to get carried away and lower the profile down to rim-protector height, never mind what it does to the handling.

The black-rubber protective strip that runs around the perimeter of the car looks rather German, too. And rather sensible, we think, given the way parking lots eat up good cars these days.

There's yet another aspect of the Mustang GT that suggests German, and that's the seating position. Detroiters are low—you have to sit on the floor—and they

have solar-cooker windshields that bake your lap and tumblehome side glass that drops rain on your ear when you crack open the window. But not in the Mustang. The extra 2.4 inches of height (compared with the IROC Camaro's) allows you to sit up. The headroom soars overhead like a cathedral—or a BMW.

Of course, none of these German suggestions would matter—we probably wouldn't even have noticed them—if the Mustang GT didn't have a German way of getting down the road. And here again Ford has done the un-American thing. Lusty Detroiters roar and rumble: their air cleaners honk, and their exhausts say 1967. But the GT is refined. The air intake is muted, and the pipes issue only a minor-key blurble, just enough to leave no doubt that there are eight cylinders hooked to the other end. The engine is a delight, eager as any German and remarkably responsive. Lug it down to 1200 rpm in fifth, and it just goes when you push the pedal. Lug it down to 800, and it falters for a fraction of a second (not to be confused with a stumble) before it goes. Just a little reminder that this is a real American V-8 under the hood, one

that hasn't succumbed to total homogenization yet, one with a *Holley carburetor*. The engine is fully up to date—all the electronics an ignition could ever ask for, roller lifters to eliminate friction, and, later in the year, a two-speed accessory drive to cut another 5 hp in parasitic losses—but all the driver notices is that it seems to produce a bountiful harvest of horsepower with no ruckus. You have to be of a certain maturity to appreciate this.

So you're sitting head high, all German-like in the front bucket of this Mustang, the engine whirring easily instead of grumbling, having a pretty nice time motoring down the blacktop, when you notice that the white-on-black speedometer says *80 mph*. The road is neglected-infrastructure rough, and you're not even gripping the wheel. In fact, you hadn't really noticed the speed, just that everything was copacetic and fun. And this, finally, blurs the last differences between Dearborn and Deutschland. This car has *dynamik*. Call it road sense. Call it German aplomb. Call it good. For sure, Mustangs have never possessed it before, and neither did the spoilered-and-skirted offerings from across town. No one advancement can be cited, just as size isn't the only difference between a kid and a grown-up.

The Mustang doesn't feel like a Detroit heavyweight. Its dimensions are spare. It has balance. The wind noise is subdued. The ride is disciplined—maybe a little on the choppy side in its vertical motions over some rough stuff but not muscle-car harsh by any means. The steering knows where straight ahead is. The rear axle is sufficiently stabilized that it doesn't launch you in surprising directions. And the car has legs. Long legs. There's always a longer gear when you need it. The Mustang GT is the kind of car that's never out of its element. You bring on the challenges. It can cope.

Several systems are worth singling out. The rear suspension is good. Finally. The four-angled-links arrangement was inherited from the Fairmont. They were short

links, okay for a cooking sedan with skinny tires, but the geometry at work back there meant extraordinary measures were required to make "GT" handling. And you know how Detroit hates extraordinary measures. But, finally, Ford came through. Gas-filled shock absorbers are used vertically, and an extra set of horizontal shocks damps axle movements in the windup direction. Once in a while you can still make the axle take an awkward step, but no longer will it dance. This is a tremendous advance for a live-axle car; in some ways, the Mustang GT now outhandles the real Germans. On a rough road, the rear wheels still aren't quite as well planted as those of a BMW, but the rigid axle gives wonderfully forgiving handling on smooth roads, with none of the *oops!* you've come to expect when you get the g-forces up in a semi-

trailing-arm car and then lift off the power. Overall, the Mustang GT can hold its own.

The gearing is a pleasure, too. For a long time after the fuel crisis, we got our performance with short axle ratios. The engines didn't have any torque, but if they were geared tightly enough, you could pretend. There is no pretense in the Mustang GT. It has a 3.08 axle ratio turning fifteen-inch tires. Fifth gear peaks at 135 mph with a nice, serene 3850 rpm on the tach. The ratios below that are perfectly matched to the torque curve. And perfectly spaced for driving pleasure. Another detail: the lever feels as though it comes right out of the top of the transmission, which it effectively does. No remote linkage to add *clunk-clunk* to the shifting process and subtract accuracy from the motion.

In general, accuracy seems a good word

The GT sounds fine, too—smoothly mechanical, not too loud, not too much intrusion from body rattles and creaks. There is just a trace of aftershake following bumps—you feel it and hear it—but when you remember that this is a hatchback with a tail that opens like the cargo bay of a C-5A, Ford's accomplishment is considerable. Two years ago no one would have believed it possible. The notchback two-door body is probably even tighter, but the GT package is not offered there. You can get a GT convertible, however.

You don't expect such refinement this late in the model cycle: the current Mustang has been around since 1979. But the Germans keep after their stock, always improving, and the German influence in Ford is being felt. It's a good thing, too, because the Mustang is going to get older still before it's replaced, probably in 1988. But if it keeps aging this gracefully, who cares?

You don't *have* to rush around in the GT, but you can. The machinery won't let you down. You probably will rush, just because the car seems so happy in its work. And that, in turn, gives you something to look forward to each afternoon, when you're ready to put down your own work. You might say it gives a new meaning to happy hour.
—*Patrick Bedard*

COUNTERPOINT

• I know, I know, the Camaro IROC-Z generates better roadholding numbers than the Mustang GT, and I vividly remember that our experts chose the Camaro over the Mustang in our "Best-Handling American Car" story. Nonetheless, if I were about to buy a car in this category, I would buy the Mustang so fast it would make your head spin. You know why? Because the Mustang is so much fun, that's why. Even with all the improvements Ford has made, even with the better-controlled rear axle, the Mustang still behaves with a kind of careless brio that makes me love it a lot more than a bunch of cars that are all numbers and not much fun. The Mustang puts the performance where you can use it—on the road, on the way to work, on your summer vacation, not screeching around a painted circle in the farthest corner of the manufacturer's proving ground. This is not just a driver's car. This is an *enthusiast* driver's car. Stab it and steer it, and laugh like a fool when the secondaries open and the trees get all blurred. —*David E. Davis, Jr.*

If the Mustang GT has been overshadowed by Chevy's Camaro IROC-Z, that's too bad, because in many ways the Ford is better.

The Mustang's handling isn't as stuck down, but it's more hospitable for most driving. It even feels pretty good when you're making it earn its keep. It tracks better than the Chevy, and, once you figure out when to mess with the steering and when to leave it alone, it may even steer better (not to say quicker). The GT's brakes generally feel okay, but they're seriously squooshy in hard use, a potentially grim flaw. And its engine is coldblooded, sometimes surges

below 2000 rpm, and starves for fuel in hard right-handers. Despite these woes, the V-8 is strong and revvy, and, like the clutch and the shifter, it feels surprisingly slick, even sophisticated. The cockpit fits an active driver's needs. The visibility, the seats, the pedals, the shifter, the wheel, and the gauges are right. When you're annoyed by the know-nothing steering or the lively axle or the spongy brakes, at least you're properly set to see to business, and that's good, because this car is one fast piece of business.
—*Larry Griffin*

Perseverance pays off. In this case, perseverance is spelled Donald Petersen, the president of the Ford Motor Company and also the man who was eager to make year-by-year installments toward the mechanical perfection of the Mustang. Although the perfect car hasn't yet been built, Ford's horsepower pony is clearly getting better with age. This year, the hot engine, the slick-shifting five-speed, and the reasonably capable chassis seem to like one another a lot. There's an honest mechanical harmony that prevails throughout the whole car.

I'm especially impressed by the maturity that has come to the rear axle. It was born with one locating link missing—a situation that hampered the Mustang in any confrontation with its arch rival from Chevrolet for years. But now, thanks to a total of four shock absorbers to damp out the occasional miscues of the four rear locating links (instead of the more desirable five), the fat tires that have been added for 1985 actually have a chance to stick to the pavement. The Camaro may be a better handler, but for sheer fun, I'd throw my saddle on the Mustang.
—*Don Sherman*

to describe the GT's behavior. It has an almost reflexive way of doing what you want, going where you aim. Which reminds us that there are two kinds of handling: the kind at which the GT excels, as well as the more academic kind, which manifests itself in comparison numbers. On the skidpad, the GT is very good—0.79 g is certainly nothing to be embarrassed about—but it's a bit short of today's best, though certainly more than a match for any German sedan. The Mustang's numbers are compromised by too much understeer. Most folks, however, won't notice.

Maybe the most important point to make in all this talk about German characteristics is that you don't have to rush around in the GT to get your money's worth. It sits fine, head high, as we've mentioned; and, appropriately, a pair of serious buckets intended especially for coping with lateral forces have been included as standard equipment. Skinny guys are going to rattle around in them a bit more than they'd like, but then skinny guys have the same problem with off-the-rack shirts as well.

Vehicle type: front-engine, rear-wheel-drive, 4-passenger, 3-door sedan

Price as tested: $11,391

Options on test car: base Ford Mustang GT, $9885; air conditioning, $743; power windows, $198; power door locks, $177; rear defroster, $140; premium sound system, $138; tilt steering wheel, $110.

Sound system: AM/FM-stereo radio, 4 speakers, 24 watts per channel

ENGINE
Type .... V-8, iron block and heads
Bore x stroke .... 4.00 x 3.00 in, 101.6 x 76.2mm
Displacement .... 302 cu in, 4942cc
Compression ratio 8.3:1
Carburetion .... 1x4-bbl Holley
Emissions controls .....3-way catalytic converter, feedback
fuel-air-ratio control, EGR, auxiliary air pump
Valve gear .... pushrods, hydraulic lifters
Power (SAE net) .... 210 bhp @ 4600 rpm
Torque (SAE net) .... 265 lbs-ft @ 3400 rpm
Redline .... 5800 rpm

DRIVETRAIN
Transmission 5-speed
Final-drive ratio .... 3.08:1, limited slip

Gear	Ratio	Mph/1000 rpm	Max. test speed
I	3.35	7.1	39 mph (5500 rpm)
II	1.93	12.4	68 mph (5500 rpm)
III	1.29	18.5	102 mph (5500 rpm)
IV	1.00	23.9	131 mph (5500 rpm)
V	0.68	35.2	135 mph (3850 rpm)

DIMENSIONS AND CAPACITIES
Wheelbase .... 100.5 in
Track, F/R .... 56.6/57.0 in
Length .... 179.3 in
Width .... 69.1 in

Height .... 52.1 in
Frontal area .... 20.6 sq ft
Ground clearance .... 4.9 in
Curb weight .... 3167 lbs
Weight distribution, F/R 58.7/41.3%
Fuel capacity .... 15.4 gal
Water capacity .... 14.1 qt

CHASSIS/BODY
Type .... unit construction
Body material .... welded steel stampings

INTERIOR
SAE volume, front seat .... 50 cu ft
rear seat .... 34 cu ft
trunk space .... 12 cu ft
Front seats .... bucket
Recliner type .... ratchet
General comfort .... poor fair good **excellent**
Fore-and-aft support .... poor fair good **excellent**
Lateral support .... poor fair good **excellent**

SUSPENSION
F: .... ind, MacPherson strut, coil springs, anti-sway bar
R: .... rigid axle, 4 trailing links, coil springs, anti-sway bar

STEERING
Type .... rack-and-pinion, power-assisted
Turns lock-to-lock 2.5
Turning circle curb-to-curb .... 37.4 ft

BRAKES
F: .... 10.1 x 0.9-in vented disc
R: .... 9.0 x 1.8-in cast-iron drum
Power assist .... vacuum

WHEELS AND TIRES
Wheel size .... 7.0 x 15 in
Wheel type .... cast aluminum
Tires .... Goodyear Eagle VR60, P225/60VR-15
Test inflation pressures, F/R .... 30/30 psi

CAR AND DRIVER TEST RESULTS

ACCELERATION — Seconds
Zero to 30 mph 2.3
40 mph 3.5
50 mph 4.7
60 mph 6.4
70 mph 8.6
80 mph 11.1
90 mph 14.3
100 mph 18.8
Top-gear passing time, 30–50 mph 11.2
50–70 mph 11.2
Standing ¼-mile .... 14.9 sec @ 91 mph
Top speed .... 135 mph

BRAKING
70–0 mph @ impending lockup .... 206 ft
Modulation .... poor fair **good** excellent
Fade .... **none** moderate heavy
Front-rear balance .... poor fair **good**

HANDLING
Roadholding, 300-ft-dia skidpad .... 0.79 g
Understeer............ minimal moderate **excessive**

COAST-DOWN MEASUREMENTS
Road horsepower @ 50 mph .... 14.5 hp
Friction and tire losses @ 50 mph .... 6.0 hp
Aerodynamic drag @ 50 mph .... 8.5 hp

FUEL ECONOMY
EPA city driving .... **16 mpg**
EPA highway driving .... 24 mpg
C/D observed fuel economy .... **14 mpg**

INTERIOR SOUND LEVEL
Idle .... 54 dBA
Full-throttle acceleration .... 80 dBA
70-mph cruising .... 74 dBA
70-mph coasting .... 72 dBA

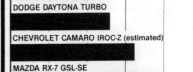

CURRENT BASE PRICE dollars x 1000

FORD MUSTANG GT
DODGE DAYTONA TURBO
CHEVROLET CAMARO IROC-Z (estimated)
MAZDA RX-7 GSL-SE
0   4   8   12   16   20

ACCELERATION seconds
■ 0–60 mph
■ ¼-mile

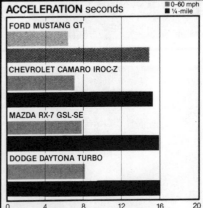

FORD MUSTANG GT
CHEVROLET CAMARO IROC-Z
MAZDA RX-7 GSL-SE
DODGE DAYTONA TURBO
0   4   8   12   16   20

70–0 MPH BRAKING feet

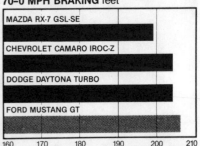

MAZDA RX-7 GSL-SE
CHEVROLET CAMARO IROC-Z
DODGE DAYTONA TURBO
FORD MUSTANG GT
160   170   180   190   200   210

EPA ESTIMATED FUEL ECONOMY mpg

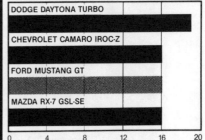

DODGE DAYTONA TURBO
CHEVROLET CAMARO IROC-Z
FORD MUSTANG GT
MAZDA RX-7 GSL-SE
0   4   8   12   16   20

INTERIOR SOUND LEVEL dBA
■ 70-mph cruise
■ Full-throttle

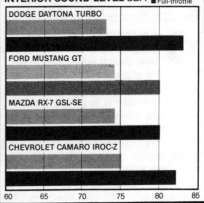

DODGE DAYTONA TURBO
FORD MUSTANG GT
MAZDA RX-7 GSL-SE
CHEVROLET CAMARO IROC-Z
60   65   70   75   80   85

The 1985½ Mustang
SVO—*Special
Velocity Option*

STEALTH FIGHTER

By Jeff Smith

Out in the desert of New Mexico, the government is working on a new stealth fighter plane that will be the slickest thing since jets replaced prop-driven fighters after World War II. The plan is to build a fighter that's nearly invisible to conventional radar. What does this have to do with late-model high-performance cars? Not much, except that a similar small group of people within Ford, known as SVO (Specialty Vehicle Operations), has come up with their own nearly invisible

version of a street stealth fighter called the 1985½ SVO. We say "nearly invisible" because the street set has never really accepted the SVO as a true performance car. Until now. After testing this little boulevard bomber, we think the Mustang's SVO intials should stand for "Special Velocity Option." Yes friends, this year they've made the SVO not only faster than last year's model—but for $1100 less than the base price of the '84!

Let's lay out the facts. The SVO was

designed as a low-production supercar to showcase Ford's commitment to four-cylinder performance as the powerplant of the future. To this end, the SVO has always been, and probably always will be, a four-cylinder performance car. However, the SVO has also had to overcome the negative bias produced by Ford's initial foray into turbocharged four cylinders with the 1979 carbureted 2.3 motor, which was disappointing. But no more. The SVO lays to waste the idea that a four-lunger can't run. As evidence, how about 15.10/91.55 mph corrected times at Los Angeles County Raceway? Uncorrected the car still ran 15.35/90.00 mph at 2700 feet altitude all day long. According to our sister book, *Motor Trend*, the best a 1984 SVO could muster was a 15.85/87.40, which makes the '85½ SVO a solid .75-second and 4.15 mph faster!

For anyone familiar with the '84 SVO, the '85½ version feels like it has 30 more horsepower—which it does. The '84 spec'd out at 176 hp, while the '85½ charges in at *205 hp* and *248 lbs./ft.* of torque. Where did all this wondrous power come from? Actually, a number of revisions were responsible for this power surge. First, the intake manifold was redesigned and the turbine housing was tightened up from an A/R ratio of .63 to .47 to bring the boost in sooner. While the 15-pound boost limit and air-to-air intercooler remain the same as last year, SVO did redesign the camshaft by adding 20 more degrees of intake and exhaust duration along with revising the cylinder head intake ports. They also pumped up the Bosch electronic injectors for more capacity and then reduced the exhaust backpressure by a whopping 50 percent by adding a dual exhaust system behind the single catalytic converter.

STEALTH FIGHTER

The key to the SVO's turbo power is the intercooler (arrow). The air-to-air heat exchanger reduces inlet air temperature to the engine after the turbocharger, allowing the 2.3-liter engine to make 15 pounds of boost and an astounding 205 hp!

Nimble doesn't begin to tell the tale of the SVO's responsiveness. The lightweight four-cylinder makes this 'Stang a super handler. Of course, P225/60VR16 Goodyear gatorbacks don't hurt.

The first thing you notice on the '85½ SVO is the flush-mounted headlights. These aren't headlight covers, but true aerodynamic headlights.

All of these changes, along with a stronger clutch, revised transmission ratios, and a 3.73 rear gear combine to make the '85½ SVO a very strong package. As a matter of fact, we had a chance to stage an impromptu side-by-side 0-60 duel with an '84 SVO during our test. The '85½ quickly put two car lengths on the earlier Mustang before we got out of second gear.

Unlike last year's SVO, the boost comes on much sooner in the '85½, making the power surge less like a "light switch" action. This makes driving the new SVO in traffic an absolute thrill, since the boost kicks in almost at will. The dreaded "turbo lag" is certainly a thing of the past with the '85½ SVO, even at the dragstrip. The key to obtaining good e.t.'s with the new SVO is to leave at about 3500 rpm. This spins the tires about 10 feet out. Then the tires hook up, the boost kicks in, and the tires break loose—making the car feel like a scaled down version of a Funny Car.

Of course the other half of this stealth fighter's performance is its exceptionally superb cornering response. After our first pass down our Mulholland mountain test course, we got out to look for the slot car peg under the front bumper. While it obviously doesn't have one, the combination of the

The interior is basically unchanged from last year. The shifter has been tightened up with shorter throws and the ignition retard switch has been retained for bouts with bad gas.

P225/60VR16 Goodyear gatorback tires and revised shock valving and spring rates only improve the SVO's already nimble handling.

So what's the bottom line? Just this. The '85½ SVO is not only faster and less expensive than a year ago, it also has more usable power. And to the performance skeptics who discount the car because it's only a four-cylinder, we can only say this—don't be too cocky with your small-block supercar. It's hard to save face when you've just been snookered by a four-cylinder SVO! ⓖ

Camaro IROC-Z
vs.
Mustang SVO

How can such a tiny motor go so fast?

by Ron Grable
PHOTOGRAPHY BY JIM BROWN

This head-to-head confrontation is critical to the mental health of all Red-Blooded American Males (RBAMs). Ranks right up there with periodic doses of baseball, apple pie, Mom, and letters from home. What we've got here are *the* two American GT cars. There are other pretenders to this lofty All-American GT perch, but RBAMs don't drive cars that spin their front tires. RBAMs also drive V-8s, right? Whoops, not so clear on that one. The V-8 still has its seductive qualities, but it uses too much fuel to produce that wonderful torque. Which is why RBAMs are showing up these days behind smaller engines producing just as much power at higher efficiencies: V-6s, inline fours, turbocharging, intercooling, electronic engine management, direct port injection, and four valves per cylinder are all means to the future direction in small, powerful, efficient powerplants. So this comparison will contrast the been-around-for-a-long-time V-8 approach with a high-tech small-engined muscle car of comparable performance.

In the All-American GT scheme of things, real men don't drive cars that spin their front tires

Chevrolet offers the top-of-the-line IROC-Z in two engine/transmission configurations, a carbureted 5.0-liter V-8 with 5-speed manual, or the electronic fuel-injected induction system version in front of a 4-speed automatic with overdrive. The EFI V-8 probably qualifies as medium tech, because the sophisticated injection system is actually state-of-the-art hardware, but the basic 5.0-liter V-8 is in the twilight of its useful life. It has been massaged and coaxed year after year into producing acceptable fuel efficiencies, but the engineers will privately admit that with the EPA looking over their shoulders, and the ongoing pressure of CAFE (Corporate Average Fuel Economy), its days are numbered. Most of their energies are currently directed at V-6 technology.

We chose the carbureted 5-speed version of the IROC-Z for this comparison, partly because of its "low-tech" approach to the business of a GT car, and partly because that's the only way the excellent 5-speed manual transmission is available. (Thank you, CAFE.) We felt it necessary that both cars be equipped with manual transmissions, because automatics are generally sneered at by true RBAMs, and because we wanted to make sure we were comparing apples with apples here. However, since the big news for the IROC line this year is the Tuned Port-Injection system (also available on the Corvette), we have included the performance data (and some technical information) for an auto-transmissioned EFI IROC-Z in the accompanying sidebar.

The SVO represents Ford's future-tech American GT, at least under the hood. (Also, as we hinted earlier, we still feel a true performance GT needs rear-wheel drive.) Its performance envelope is similar to other GTs (Ford's own 5.0-liter versions included), but it manages to be competitive using a "small" 2.3-liter inline four, with exhaust turbocharging, intercooling, and electronic management of most engine parameters like fuel injection, boost, and ignition timing. So let's begin with a detailed look at what each manufacturer offers.

For '85½, Ford's SVO has had a number of evolutionary changes aimed specifically at refining the breed, first introduced in late 1983. Without question the most important improvements, from a potential buyer's standpoint, are the improved engine characteristics. Probably the most common complaint heard about the earlier SVOs was the "buzzy" nature of the engine. The motor transmitted all manner of vibrations to the driver. When the engine was being used hard, the steering wheel, gear lever, pedals, mirrors—seemingly everything—vibrated in a concert of resonating frequencies. There didn't seem to be any point on the tach where the 4-banger was happy, and this naturally detracted from the enjoyment of the car.

The '85½ edition of this Ford engine is a night-to-day improvement. It develops more power, more torque, is an order of magnitude smoother, and is great fun to drive. How dey do dat,

A lower stance, Goodyear "gatorbacks," and increased torsional and lateral stability results in a sticky 0.87g skidpad ride.

you say? Well, according to the SVO engine people it was pretty simple. On the way to upgrading engine power, a few simple changes in the intake manifold and stiffening the front bracketry (for air conditioning, power steering, alternator, etc.) significantly reduced engine NVH—noise, vibration, and harshness. Apparently the intake manifold and ancillary equipment were the major source of the vibration because this redesign is silky smooth compared to the earlier version.

This year's 30 additional horsepower comes from changes to the turbo system and internal hot-rodding to increase airflow. A new camshaft profile generates quicker valve opening

rates, 20° more intake/exhaust duration, and 20° more overlap. The intake valve profile has been reshaped, and the new stiffer intake manifold has been contoured to flow more air. To take advantage of the engine's ability to flow more air, backpressure was reduced 50% with an inline catalyst and dual exhaust muffler, and the turbo was reconfigured to reduce the A/R ratio approximately 23%. The A/R ratio (turbine blade area divided by the radius to the center of pressure for that area) is a basic measure of the responsiveness of the turbo. Numerically reducing the ratio as Ford has done works to increase responsiveness by accelerating the turbine faster, which, of course, com-

presses the intake charge quicker—less turbo lag.

Since the engine is capable of processing more air, it requires a similar increase in fuel flow, so the injector nozzles were upgraded to 35 lb/hr compared to the '84 system's 30 lb/hr. For '85½, the wastegate control was integrated with EEC-IV (previously done by a separate module), and different control parameters were established for boost, up 1.0 psi to 15.0.

The chassis changes for '85 were minimal but productive. The overall handling feel of the new SVO is sig-

nificantly improved, due in part to the faster steering ratio—15:1 compared to last year's 20:1. Steering effort was kept the same as before, and the combination is excellent, with good on-center response and road feel. Shock valving was tightened up slightly, and Teflon-lined front anti-roll bar bushings were used to reduce "stiction." Stiction comes from sticking-friction, and is characterized by the force required to initiate small displacements. When large displacements are involved, friction is determined by the sliding parameters between the two surfaces, but with limited displacements an initial sticking is involved, which increases the force required to initiate motion. When small bumps or irregularities are spaced close together (such as freeway expansion grooves), the anti-roll bar can impart a false stiffness to the chassis by virtue of the stiction of its bushings. Ford's SVO Teflon linings combat this tendency. While this may seem a small item, it allows the chassis engineers to trade off more aggressive shock valving against the reduced anti-roll bar contribution to chassis stiffness, without putting too much harshness in the ride quality.

Car nuts are demanding owners, and subjective feel is very important in how they relate to their cars. Ford has made some subtle changes to promote the tight-coupled feel so prized in performance vehicles, and the results are impressive. The Hurst people reworked the shift linkage on the Borg-Warner T-5 and relocated the lever rearward slightly. The reduced throw and effort transform the whole perception of the car—it's now a "wrist-shifter," requiring only a flick of the wrist to engage any gear you need. In line with this philosophy, the clutch throw was also reduced, and the combination of faster steering, precise shifting, and accurate clutch engagement reward the driver who appreciates such distinctions.

The exterior of the '85½ SVO remains unchanged with the small but significant exception of the flush aero headlights. The biplane spoiler, asymmetrical hood scoop, wheel spats ahead of the rear wheel arches, and rounded aero-nose still try their damndest to modernize the long-in-the-tooth Mustang. And to some extent they partially succeed—but not entirely. Underneath these licks, the boxy vertical profile is looking more dated each year, and is long overdue for a major facelift, though this isn't scheduled until 1987.

The big news in the Camaro lineup

A most refined SVO comes from 30 additional horses, a stiffer suspension, quicker steering, and a more precise shift linkage.

for 1985 is the added-at-the-top IROC-Z. As mentioned earlier, we chose to use the carbureted L-69 version for this comparison, ahead of the manual 5-speed. Exterior changes abound for the IROC-Z. To name a few: fog lamps in the grille opening, deeper front spoiler, ground-effects rocker panels, new rear bumper treatment, and hood louvers. Standard equipment (read no choice) includes lots of body decals to remind you what you bought, and interior graphics to remind you again after you're inside. The F-body (Camaro/Firebird) is one of the nicest things General Motors has done for us in years, but we just hate to see these annual "image enhancements."

The L-69 version of the 5.0-liter V-8 is second to the TPI in terms of power, using a single 800 CFM Rochester 4-throat carburetor. The 4-bbl has been around long enough to be fairly trouble-free, but at anything under three eighths of a tank, minor fuel starvation occurred during hard cornering.

The '85 IROC-Z has undergone some chassis twiddling by the F-car engineers, to keep it firmly at the top of the Camaro lineup. First, the car is 15 mm (0.59 in.) lower than the Z28, which adds up to a lower cg. Lowering the car also decreases available suspension travel, so higher-rate bump rubbers were needed to control wheel motion near the limit of travel, and shock valving was tightened up slightly. Testing early in the IROC-Z program indicated some flexure in the front structure, so a subframe was designed—to increase torsional and lateral stiffness—that incorporated the anti-roll bar. Steering effort was increased for more road feel, and steering lock reduced to accommodate the larger 245/50VR16 Gatorback tires. The Goodyears needed a click more positive caster (to 4°) for increased straight-line stability and aligning torque. At the rear, the anti-roll bar was increased 1 mm (to 24 mm) to reduce understeer (we love it), and Bilstein gas shocks were fitted.

At the track we found that both cars have strengths and weaknesses, as expected, but the suprising thing is how closely matched they are. A look at the data panels shows the two cars are nearly identical in every performance category, the Camaro doing 0-60 almost a half second quicker, and the SVO lapping the racetrack in 0.69 sec less than its GM counterpart. But the numbers tell only a small portion of the story. For instance, after lapping both cars around the track, we were

convinced we had gone much faster in the SVO, strictly due to the sensations transmitted to the driver. At full-kill in the SVO, lots of things are happening. The turbo is whining and whistling up and down its rev spectrum, there is a strange distinctive squeal from the compressor as it works on the incoming charge, the wastegate whooshes and clicks as it vents the exhaust pressure, all played over the turbo-muted hum of the exhaust. All conspire to give the impression of lots of activity. The underhood intensity, combined with lots of shifting to keep this little baby up in the power range, convinces you that you've just broken the absolute track record.

Contrasted with the SVO, the IROC-Z sort of rumbles around the track feeling entirely unconcerned about what gear you happen to have it in or how many revs it's turning. Acceleration just depends on how deep your foot is in the throttle—there always seems to be adequate torque on demand. The engine sound doesn't change very much, and the exhaust note is the only sound audible over the howl of tortured tires.

At the conclusion of the track portion of the test, both cars had lapped at very similar times, in spite of their wildly divergent personalities. The Ford was fastest when it was driven in anger, and the Chevy didn't seem to care how it was driven, it was always just as fast.

From a chassis dynamics standpoint, both cars are quite well balanced and suited for "spirited" driving. The SVO's slightly faster speed around the track is a reflection of the 15-hp advantage it enjoys over the IROC-Z, combined with brakes that are better balanced. The Chevy has a little too much rear brake bias, as well as too much assist; drive too deep into a corner and the rears will lock up, usually with spectacular results, so the proper technique is moderate early braking.

Braking distances and skidpad times slightly favor the Camaro, attributable to its larger tire/wheel combination, and the IROC's slalom advantage is due to the instantaneous torque available to accelerate between gates. Acceleration for the quarter mile points out the difference between turbo power and lots of cubic inches. The SVO was more difficult to launch, reflected in its slower 0-60 time, but at the end of the strip it had almost caught up (only 0.05 sec slower), indicative of its more favorable power-to-weight ratio.

Living with these two in day-to-day commuting emphasizes the different approaches to the job of Grand Touring. The nod for carving up daily traffic would go to the IROC-Z. The instant-on torque lets you squirt through any hole with ease, while the SVO requires a little rowing with the gear lever to slip into the same opening, and is also slower out of the

---

DATA

Chevrolet Camaro IROC-Z

POWERTRAIN
Vehicle configuration	Front engine, rear drive
Engine configuration	V-8, OHV, 2 valves/cylinder
Displacement	4988 cc (305 cu in.)
Max. power (SAE net)	190 hp @ 4800 rpm
Max. torque (SAE net)	240 lb-ft @ 3200 rpm
Transmission	5-sp. man.
Axle ratio	3.73:1

CHASSIS
Suspension, f/r	Independent/live axle
Brakes, f/r	Disc/disc
Steering	Recirculating ball
Wheels	16 x 8.0 in., alloy
Tires	P245/50VR16

DIMENSIONS
Wheelbase	2556 mm (101.5 in.)
Overall length	4877 mm (192.0 in.)
Curb weight	1497 kg (3300 lb)
Fuel capacity	58.7 L (15.5 gal)

PERFORMANCE
0-60 mph	6.87 sec
Standing quarter mile	15.32 sec/89.6 mph
Braking, 60-0	138 ft
Lateral acceleration	0.87 g
Slalom	6.46 sec
Racetrack	1:27.42

DATA

Ford Mustang SVO

POWERTRAIN
Vehicle configuration	Front engine, rear drive
Engine configuration	L-4, OHC, 2 valves/cylinder
Displacement	2301 cc (140 cu in.)
Max. power (SAE net)	205 hp @ 5000 rpm
Max. torque (SAE net)	248 lb-ft @ 3000 rpm
Transmission	5-sp. man.
Axle ratio	3.45:1

CHASSIS
Suspension, f/r	Independent/live axle
Brakes, f/r	Disc/disc
Steering	Rack and pinion
Wheels	16 x 7.0 in., alloy
Tires	P225/50VR16

DIMENSIONS
Wheelbase	2552 mm (100.5 in.)
Overall length	4597 mm (181.0 in.)
Curb weight	1380 kg (3036 lb)
Fuel capacity	58.3 L (15.4 gal)

PERFORMANCE
0-60 mph	7.23 sec
Standing quarter mile	15.37 sec/89.4 mph
Braking, 60-0	140 ft
Lateral acceleration	0.85 g
Slalom	6.66 sec
Racetrack	1:26.73

blocks when the light turns green. Creature comforts are comparable, but seating in the SVO offers more adjustment for six-footers. The Camaro seat is too high off the floorpan, requiring a severe angle for the seatback to obtain adequate head room.

Sustained high-speed touring (55 mph and up) in both cars is very pleasant, with only a few notations on the negative side of the ledger. The Camaro's deep, throaty exhaust rumble, for example, can get tiring after a long time at open-road speeds, although the SVO activity under the hood also intrudes under the same circumstances. Both cars demonstrate good high-speed stability, but the Camaro is a little more sensitive to road irregularities, bordering on twitchy under some conditions. This results from the combination of large, sticky tires and stiff suspension components. Chevy's Camaro engineering team stacked its chips behind a program designed to make the car as precise and responsive as possible, but an unfortunate by-product of this is some slight wandering and darting

when the wheels are moving up and down over rough surfaces. It's far from uncontrollable, but you do have to click your attention up a notch or two.

The SVO—under the same circumstances—has better directional stability. It's softer in roll, has a more compliant suspension feel, and doesn't need quite as much concentration to keep it going straight over bumpy high-speed stuff.

In the past, most American high-performance cars have labored under the cross of terminal understeer. In these two offerings from Ford and Chevrolet, we see a slight shift in that policy. They can in no way be classified as oversteerers—and rightly so—but they have certainly moved away from the total incapacitating understeer we have come to expect. Pushed to their limits, and with judicial throttle use, they will reward the driver with a controllable, nearly neutral cornering attitude. It's about time. Both of these American GTs do a good job of reducing wind noise, at least up to the 80 to 90-mph range.

Above that and some buffeting and howling is evident—cancellable with the radio volume switch.

The toughest part of this story is picking a winner. The objective data doesn't clearly point at one or the other, so it has to be a subjective choice, and those are always the most agonizing. But here goes—we like the '85½ Mustang SVO. We are mainly seduced by its high-revving, big-hearted little motor and its precise, tight-coupled controls. Its drivetrain has all the appeal of a Formula Atlantic car: intense, demanding, rewarding (when employed correctly), and *fun*. We would appreciate less suspension compliance but that's easily fixable in the aftermarket.

The IROC-Z offers a more precise suspension calibration, a little bigger tire/wheel package, and we prefer its looks, but the 5.0-liter V-8 feels "dated" after spending any time in the SVO. Let's see now, there's probably more than adequate room under that louvered IROC hood for that little 2.3-liter Ford screamer, and then we could . . . . [MT]

LB9/TPI: More Grunt Per Gallon

It offers a full 25 more horsepower with equal fuel efficiency. It's as quick and fast, but more throttle-responsive and much more fun to drive. It's the LB9 Tuned Port Injection (TPI) IROC-Z with a take-it-or-leave-it 4-speed automatic, and it's definitely a match for the carbureted 5-speed manual IROC-Z.

If nothing else, the LB9 engine is a graphic example of how fuel efficiency and power output need not be mutually exclusive, and how, through the application of more precise air/fuel management, design engineers can effect gains in *both* without the traditional reciprocal tradeoffs.

The objective of the TPI project was fuel efficiency, aimed specifically at offsetting the Corporate Average Fuel Economy (CAFE) gas-guzzler tax on Chevy's small-block V-8 engine family through 1986. To achieve this, design engineers first went to a higher-ratio rear axle (from 3.73:1 to 3.42 and 3.23), which reduced engine speed and fuel consumption across the entire band—normally a tradeoff resulting in reduced off-the-line throttle response.

To compensate for the reduction in low-end punch, and to further enhance the engine's fuel efficiency, a computer-controlled fuel delivery system was designed combining Bosch electronic fuel-injection hardware (primary injectors, cold-start injectors, and hot wire air flow meter) with a corporately designed cast aluminum air intake plenum featuring individually tuned runners for each cylin-

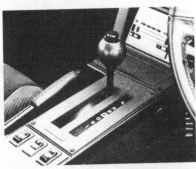

der. By fine-tuning each intake runner, engineers were able to reprogram the basic rpm formula at which the system resonated, altering the air intake pulse timing to allow horsepower to occur 400 rpm sooner in the powerband than the carbureted engine. The additional 35 lb-ft of torque—available 400 rpm sooner—more than compensated

for the higher overall gearing, resulting in comparable standing-start acceleration with the carbureted H.O. powerplant (7.43 sec 0-60, 15.93 sec at 89.3 mph quarter mile).

The hot new fuel-injected small block gets a hearty thumbs-up. Unfortunately, we feel only lukewarm about its 4-speed automatic overdrive runningmate. Deliberately programmed for low-rpm fuel efficiency, the transmission constantly wanders up and down the scale seeking the ultimate load/rpm/environment relationship. On a flat stretch of uninterrupted highway, there's no problem. But drive it up the slightest of inclines, or around tight throttle-on turns, or through congested, stop-and-go city streets, and it's downright infuriating. Jerky and imprecise with a tendency to surging on cold mornings, the shifting program can only be improved (slightly) by leaving the selector in Drive (3rd), avoiding 4th-gear Overdrive in all driving situations other than open-highway cruising.

Admittedly, it's not that the 4-speed automatic is a bad transmission. It simply does not offer a comparable—or compatible—level of performance to the fuel-injected LB9. Mild disappointment aside, the fuel-injected V-8/auto still rates as a viable alternative to the carbureted 5-speed. And although it's probably an overly optimistic assumption, it would seem logical to either improve the automatic and/or offer the 5-speed manual as an option. The engine deserves better. —*John Hanson*

PONY EXPRESS

It's the most potent production "pony" y
the 205 bhp Mustang SVO from Ford's
Special Vehicles Operation.
Howard Walker went to Detroit to drive it

It's the Rambo of the American sports car world. Tough and street-wise, it will cruise around until riled when all hell breaks loose. With all the might of a Sylvester Stallone clone, it socks a 200 bhp punch that hits you like a steam hammer.

Ford's iron-pumping Mustang SVO – unleashed to an unprepared world back in 1983 – may not have too much in the way of class but it sure has clout. Clout that will hurl it from standstill to 60 in 6.8 sec and on to a top speed of a shade under 130 mph.

It's the baby of Ford's Special Vehicles Operation headed by ex-racer Mike Kranefus – a highly modified version of Uncle Henry's near-geriatric Mustang coupé, which is likely to be put out to pasture some time next year.

The Mustang SVO is intended to breathe the last bit of fire into America's favourite "pony" and give it half a chance to fend off the latest offerings from Japanese stables with all their 16-valve and turbo offerings.

Yet there is no burbling V8 or sizzling "six" beneath the Mustang's billiard table bonnet. Instead Mr Kranefus opted for Ford's small 2.3-litre in-line four-pot engine and bolted on a turbocharger, a hefty intercooler and fuel injection system, and mated it to a five-speed Borg Warner 'box.

Not the best of choices, maybe, as many US sports car fans feel more at home driving behind the five litres of lazy V8 that power the SVO's kid brother, the Mustang GT. But Mr K. went for power and the 2.3 turbo certainly delivers, with 205 bhp on tap together with a meaty 240 lb ft of torque available low-down at 3000 rpm.

The only problem is delivery can be a bit on the slow side to start with; when you're running

200 horses all let out of the stable door at the same time cause a stampede of spinning tyres

along in fourth, push the throttle pedal deep into the Mustang's plush carpet and then wait . . . and wait. A full 30 sec can go by before the engine produces enough exhaust puff to get those turbine blades spinning.

Then whoosh, and the Mustang show gets on the road with a neck-snapping delivery of power. But goodness, does it take a long time – it brings a new standard to turbo lag. And you

The SVO is intended to breathe the last bit of fire into America's favourite pony

need all that sudden power like a hole in the head when it's pouring down with rain – 200 horses all let out of the stable door at the same time causes a stampede of spinning tyres. And if that happens on a tight turn you can expect to be watching your forward progress through the side window as the Mustang begins a neat pirouette.

The solution is to keep the turbo bubbling and the iron block engine spinning at high revs. But that becomes tiring, as the Ford lump is not the quietest when it comes to engine noise. Before long you begin to crave the lusty, low-down torque of a big V8.

But that said, the SVO certainly gets the adrenalin pumping. For when the turbo does come in, performance is exhilarating, with that 205 bhp being delivered in a hefty thump which squeezes you back into that deep hugging high-back seat. Keep the turbo spinning, snatch the next gear and acceleration really does feel blindingly quick.

Despite a suspension set-up reportedly designed by Fred Flintstone, the Mustang handles itself suprisingly well. The live rear axle – sprung by coils – is well-located by four links yet remains pretty unsophisticated. And that goes for the modified MacPherson strut set-up with the coil spring located on the lower arm.

It's at its worst driving around town; the bumps and potholes on Detroit's shady Michigan Avenue in the city's sleazy Downtown area are in danger of loosening every filling in your head as the Mustang hops and bops from one rut to the next.

The enormous bonnet scoop is pure Disneyland

Quicken the pace and the ride does smoothen out some, though this is certainly no easy rider.

We headed out of Motown towards the country haven of Ann Arbor – 60 or so miles away – in search of more demanding roads. On the twisty rural roads, the Mustang acquitted itself extremely well, cornering with poise and balance, though much of the credit probably goes to the super-grippy 225/50-section Goodyear Eagle rubber at each corner.

But that tricky mid-corner rut or pothole can cause the Mustang to leap off line, particularly in the wet, though it's not any great hardship, as a

small correction on the extreme direct power steering brings t car back into line.

And it doesn't always need pothole to cause the SVO's re end to step out of line; press t car hard into a bend and the back will gradually come roun in progressive oversteer, whic again is easily controlled. For more dramatic results, repeat same run when it's raining an snap the throttle closed mid-bend. Quick reactions tend to save the day.

While the Mustang itself is getting on in years, SVO's treatment has done wonders f

Before long you cra the lusty, low-down torque of a big V8

the appearance. The restyled front end with its flush-fitting lights and deep spoiler gives t car a mean, purposeful look. While the enormous bonnet scoop is pure Disneyland, the biplane spoiler looks as effecti on the Mustang as it did on the Sierra XR4i – but that's down t personal taste.

Inside, the Mustang has a Capri-feel about it – functional yet looking pretty dated these days. Everything falls easily to hand, though, and that leather clad steering wheel is so thick you start to wonder whether yo can get your hands around it.

The seat suited me fine; there plenty of side and back suppor to hold you in place, though the cushion felt a little flat. The thic chunky gearlever is also within easy reach and slots around its well-defined gate as easily as a hot knife slices through Lurpak.

While flat-out the Mustang w top 130 mph, most owners wou never actually find out, as the speed-shy speedo only register a maximum of 85 mph.

In the States, the Mustang SV would cost the equivalent of around £10,000 which puts it in the price bracket occupied by the Audi Coupé GT and the Mitsubishi Starion. What the Ford gains in outright, neck-snapping performance, it loses build quality. The car I drove shook and rattled and the doors shut with an unsatisfying "clang".

If the Mustang is the pinnacle of Ford's sports car muscle in th US, it would be interesting to see how the good ol' 2.8-litre Capri would fare across the pond. I know which I'd choose.

'87 models

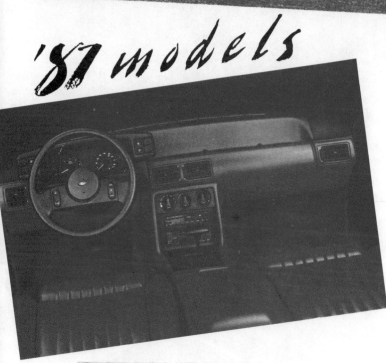

FORD MUSTANG GT

A revised profile moves the five-liter hatchback beyond the traditional Mustang look. Its new cosmetics and new interior freshen the appearance as the nameplate enters its twenty-third year on a rear-wheel-drive, two-plus-two coupe. From the front, the GT is clean and unmistakable, although the vented sills and the broadly louvered taillights seem excessive. (The more reserved Mustang LX does not inherit most of the spacey GT baubles.)

Even if you don't care for its cheese-grater taillights, there's more to love about the 1987 GT. Output has been boosted from 200 bhp to an invigorating 225 at 4400 rpm (five fewer horses and a 4000-rpm peak with the automatic transmission), courtesy of new cylinder heads and changes to the multiport fuel injection system.

The GT is still FoMoCo's finest performer. Do you like a wide torque spread? We pushed an automatic-equipped GT from walking speed to over 120 mph, all in second gear, and the engine could scarcely have been any more comfortable with the task.

With either transmission—automatic or standard five-speed manual—hurling the GT around the proving ground was lots of fun, and so was cruising back to Dearborn at day's end. The cars always felt balanced and poised and weren't unduly punishing to live with, despite their very taut suspension setups. The basic shape may be getting long in the tooth, especially viewed alongside GM's sleek Camaro and Firebird competitors, but there's life in the old horse yet.

FORD MUSTANG GT

VS

The perennial Ford-Chevy battle continue

PHOTOS BY JOE RUSZ

CHEVROLET CAMARO IROC-Z

with a 225-bhp GT vs a 220-bhp IROC-Z

THE BLACK CAMARO was a distant speck as it came off the wall-of-death banking at Ohio's Transportation Research Center. Its size grew with the approaching whoosh of air; this wasn't a car driving past so much as an aircraft buzzing our small group. The whoosh became WHOOSH as the Camaro approached as fast as something in Col Kadafi's worst nightmare, then disappeared. Only the timing lights in front of us could testify that the Camaro was ever there, its appearance was so brief. The result: 149.20 mph. Only a few minutes before, the 1987 Mustang GT had recorded 148.10 mph. The muscle cars have grown up.

We were at TRC for the first component of our comparison: The Chevrolet Camaro IROC, a with new-for-1987 350-cu-in. V-8 borrowed from the Corvette, vs the Mustang with its more pow-

erful than ever 302 and revised bodywork. Top speed was the first test and the closeness of the results would persist through tests of acceleration, handling and subjective evaluations. These two have been polished by 20 years of competition between them on city streets and race tracks of every size and shape.

Despite the similarity of results, the Mustang and Camaro achieve their performance in markedly different ways. The current Mustang has grown up in size and scale. Its history started in 1965 when it began the class known as ponycars. It grew several times until it was replaced by the Pinto-based Mustang II in 1974, which then was replaced by the compact current Mustang in 1979. Since then the Mustang has had power and suspension added; the car has become an overachiever.

For 1987 this version has undergone its most complete revision, with new bodywork front and rear. The flush headlights and below-bumper air intake are purposeful and clean, though the louvered taillight covers are, for many people, on the wrong side of stunning. A new interior replaces the blocky-looking assembly of the past with the same sort of rounded, smooth-molded shapes found on most newer Fords.

Most important of all, of course, is the 225 bhp at 4400 rpm from the well honed 5.0-liter. To add 25 bhp this year, Ford has reverted to the pre-1986 cylinder heads that allow for better airflow but less turbulence. Our test car had the 5-speed manual transmission. A 4-speed automatic is available if one is willing to sacrifice 5 bhp consumed in the automatic's more restrictive exhaust. Much larger front discs (10.9- versus 10.1-in. diameter) from the Continental add stopping power. The chassis was been subtly modified with a higher roll center, more caster and different camber settings at the modified MacPherson struts. The live axle in back on trailing and angled upper arms is unchanged this year with four shocks still holding things more or less in place.

The Camaro, which began two years after the first Mustang, has remained, if you will, a full-size ponycar, despite its slight reduction in bulk when it was restyled in 1982 for the third time. It is longer, lower and wider than the Mustang and 220 lb heavier. All of this is noticeable.

For 1987 Chevy (and Pontiac with the Firebird Trans Am) will finally, and officially, install the Corvette's 5.7-liter V-8, but with updated cast iron cylinder heads and roller valve lifters. The only available transmission is the 4-speed automatic, also shared with the Corvette. With the Camaro's lovely sounding but more restrictive exhaust, the engine produces 220 bhp at 4200 rpm and mighty 320 lb-ft at 3200 rpm. To take this increased torque, Borg-Warner rear axle (with a 3.27:1 the only available ratio) installed, along with the disc brakes that attach to the ends of the axle. No changes were made to the IROC-Z's modified MacPherson strut front suspension, except for an increase in caster, or the rear suspension's collection of lower trailing arms, torque arm and Panhard rod.

Acceleration results were as predictable as a sunrise. If, instead of comparing the Ford and Chevy, we had tested either two Mustangs or two Camaros, we would have gotten results no closer. Up to 90 mph the Mustang pulls out only the slightest advantage because of its lower weight. This disappears by 100 mph as the Camaro gains an aerodynamic advantage of the tiniest proportion. Mustang and Camaro drivers will be able to spend entire days making runs at a dragstrip without determining a clear winner, which should make for lots of happy drag racers and spectators.

There is a clear difference in technique, however, because of the Camaro's automatic transmission and the Mustang's 5-speed. Basically, the Camaro doesn't need technique. Just stand on it. The Mustang, of course, gives the driver a choice of 5-speed or automatic, and it's great fun to play with the round, black knob between the seats, though getting off the line right requires the right combination of clutch slipping, tire slipping and throttle mashing.

With the test gear still hooked up, the brakes were exercised

The Camaro retains its mechanical-looking, but efficient, arrangement of instruments, controls and seats. It's tight but attractive.

Camaro's optional L98 engine is essentially the Corvette power plant but with cast iron cylinder heads. It's strong but not silent.

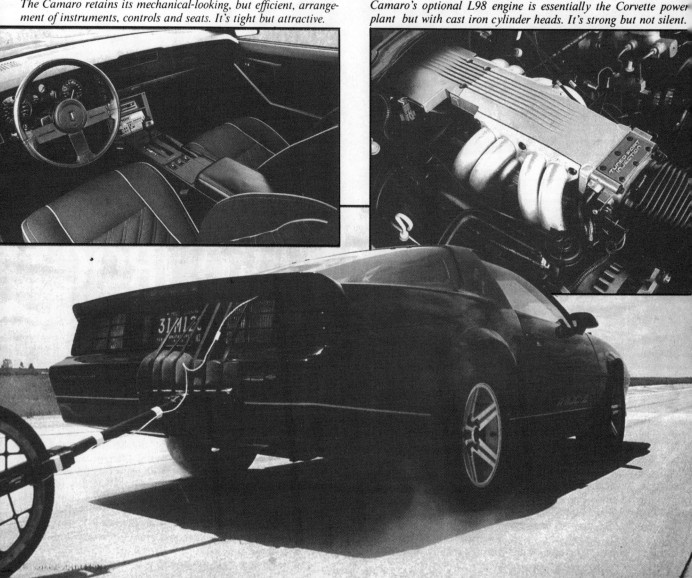

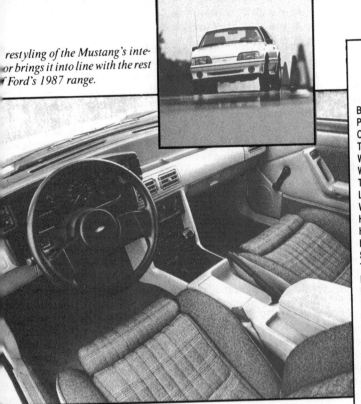

...restyling of the Mustang's interior brings it into line with the rest of Ford's 1987 range.

It may give away 50 cu in. in displacement, but the Mustang engine makes up for it with plenty of power and light weight.

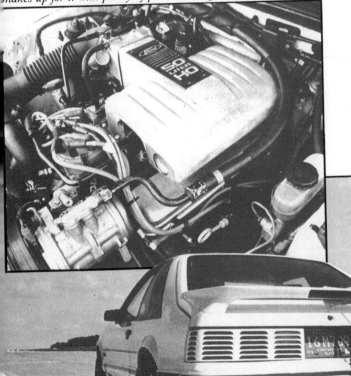

GENERAL DATA

	Chevrolet Camaro IROC-Z L98	Ford Mustang GT
Base price[1]	$12,675	$11,324
Price as tetsed[2]	$18,179	$12,548
Curb weight, lb	3490	3270
Test weight	3720	3500
Weight distribution, f/r, %	58/42	57/43
Wheelbase, in.	101.0	100.5
Track, f/r	60.7/60.6	56.6/57.0
Length	192.0	179.3
Width	72.8	69.1
Height	50.3	52.1
Head room, f/r	36.5/33.5	38.0/32.5
Leg room, f/r	43.0/21.5	43.5/23.0
Seat width, f/r	2 x 21.0/2 x 20.5	2 x 19.0/50.5
Trunk volume, cu ft	5.8+9.1	10.3+15.7
Engine type	ohv V-8	ohv V-8
Bore x stroke, mm	101.6 x 88.4	101.6 x 76.2
Displacement, cc	5733	4942
Compression ratio	9.0:1	9.0:1
Bhp @ rpm, SAE net	220 @ 4200	225 @ 4400
Torque @ rpm, lb-ft	320 @ 3200	300 @ 3000
Fuel injection	GM Tuned Port	Ford Multi Port
Fuel capacity, gal.	15.5	15.4
Transmission	4-sp automatic	5-sp manual
Gear ratios, :1	1.8 x 3.06/3.06/ 1.63/1.00/0.70	3.35/1.93/ 1.29/1.00/0.68
Final drive ratio, :1	3.27	3.08
Steering type	recirc ball, power assist	rack & pinion, power assist
Brake system, f/r	10.5-in. vented disc/ 10.5-in. vented disc	10.9-in. vented discs/ 9.0 x 1.8-in. drums
Wheels	cast alloy, 16 x 8	cast alloy, 15 x 7
Tires	Goodyear Eagle VR50, P245/50VR-16	Goodyear Eagle VR60 P225/60VR-15
Suspension	modified MacPherson struts, lower A-arms, separate coil springs, tube shocks, anti-roll bar/live axle on trailing arms, torque arms & Panhard rod; coil springs, tube shocks, anti-roll bar	modified MacPherson struts, lower A-arms, separate coil springs, tube shocks, anti-roll bar/live axle on angled upper & lower trailing arms, coil springs, dual tube shocks, anti-roll bar

[1] All prices shown are our 1987 estimates based on 1986 data.
[2] Price as tested includes: For the Camaro, 5.7-liter engine ($975), air cond ($806), IROC pkg incl wheels, tires, fog lights, trim ($695), AM/FM stereo/cassette ($571), 4-sp automatic ($510), custom cloth seats ($373), elect. adj seat ($250), elect. window lifts ($218), rear disc brakes ($186), cruise control ($182), central locking ($151), rear window heat ($151), tinted glass ($125), misc options ($311); for the Mustang, air cond ($765), AM/FM stereo/cassette ($306), rear window heat ($153).

Here, the Camaro gained some ground. It has larger tires and a better proportioning of braking force, which provided slightly shorter stopping distances. The Mustang locked the rear brakes at the initiation of braking and then locked the fronts as the car slowed to a stop. This might also prove that four disc brakes are better than two discs and two drums.

Our handling tests were reminiscent of Galileo's gravity experiments. You remember Galileo. By throwing a couple of different-weight chunks from some predecessor of the Empire State Building, he proved that an aluminum cylinder head and a cast iron cylinder head would both fall at the same rate. He would have loved the 700-ft slalom in which the fat-tired, stiffly sprung Camaro went through the cones at almost the same speed as the smaller, more loosely suspended Mustang. It was a match of the Mustang's superior steering precision vs the Camaro's tighter chassis. The 0.3-mph difference borders on insignificant.

But on a tighter than usual 150-ft skidpad the Camaro's larger tires helped it around at a higher lateral acceleration, 0.85 to 0.80. The Camaro's front suspension geometry may also be less troubled by the tight radius.

A sound test added numbers to what we all knew. The Mustang is quieter at most cruising speeds but makes more noise at wide-open throttle. If there were a number for sound quality, the Camaro would win hands down. The Chevy V-8 is tuned to produce that particularly American burble emitted by every V-8 that was ever given a set of dual pipes and glass packs. It's wonderful. At more than 125 mph, though, the side windows of the Camaro are sucked out, increasing its noise level. The Mustang remains tight all the way up.

Imagine that. A hundred and forty-eight miles in an hour. That's a Ferrari speed. And, it's the slower of the two by—once again—the smallest of margins. As impressive is the stability of both cars at those speeds. While our mighty Engineering Editor was whistling around the 7.5-mile bowl every 3.0 minutes, he was able casually to push the button of the 2-way radio and tell us the water temperature was normal, as was the oil pressure. On the back straight he had occasion to play groundhog-evasion at about 145 mph. The groundhog lost. The rpm on the Camaro, he said, was 4500 in the corners, rising to 4600 by the timing lights. The Ford was geared taller with the 5-speed and was running only 4200 rpm in 5th gear.

Now for a story. As it happened, our prototype Mustang GT (one of only two in existence) was manned by Product Development Engineer Arch Cothran when it arrived at TRC. After the 148-mph lap, Cothran calmly said, "It'll go faster in 4th." Now here was a man with confidence in his product. The message was duly relayed to our driver, who has something of a penchant for the big numbers himself. Rpm was climbing in 4th, he said from the far side of the track, hitting 5800, then more. The needle was somewhere very close to the 5900-rpm redline, he said, when the funny noises began. That was the end of that engine, an engine that had been through many hard miles of magazine and Ford testing. It died 100 yards short of the groundhog. A tie, almost.

Our testing was completed at Ford's Romeo proving ground north of Detroit with a fresh engine. No more problems. It was here that we got to romp along Woodward Avenue in a hulking IROC Camaro and a gleaming streak of a Mustang GT. On the frost bulges of Michigan's back roads, the Mustang, we discovered, provided a noticeably better ride. The Mustang also was the better commuter car of the two, with its more useful back seat and slightly taller posture. Its seats fit a wider range of drivers, though it lacked the Camaro's electric adjustment. On Ford's handling course, the Camaro was more enjoyable to drive. It's more stable under braking and those King Kong Goodyears have more traction. The Mustang is more skittish, but handles big dips better, especially the kind that bottom the Camaro's front end.

Throughout several days of testing our people kept asking one another which car was better. It was easy to hop into one and just *know* it was the grandest car on the road. The Mustang did this with its nimble, fighter-like response and sudden bursts of acceleration. In convenience and utility the Mustang offers advantages. The Camaro was equally satisfying with its unflappable handling, its soul-stirring throb and its styling that remains a work of art. To sit in the Camaro and look out past the purposeful dash, over one of the most sensuously curved hoods in existence, is a treat.

Forced to make a choice, our trio picked the Camaro when cost was no object but had fits of sensibility, not to say a split decision, when the Chevy's higher price was considered. The decision wasn't easy; the cars are as close in appeal as they are in performance. So, when it comes to the fastest 4-place cars built in America, you pretty much get what you pay for. But, in either case, you get a lot.

PERFORMANCE

	Chevrolet Camaro IROC-Z L98	Ford Mustang GT
Acceleration:		
Time to distance, sec:		
0–100 ft	3.2	3.2
0–500 ft	8.2	8.3
0–1320 ft (¼ mi)	15.3	15.3
Speed at end of ¼ mi, mph	90.5	93.0
Time to speed, sec:		
0–30 mph	2.3	2.3
0–60 mph	6.8	6.7
0–80 mph	11.8	11.5
0–100 mph	18.4	18.8
Top speed, mph	149	148
Brakes:		
Stopping distances from:		
60 mph	159	168
80 mph	261	289
Overall brake rating	good	fair
Handling:		
Lateral acceleration,[1] g	0.85	0.80
Slalom speed, mph	63.3	63.6
Interior noise, dBA:		
Idle in neutral	58	56
Maximum, 1st gear	76	79
Constant 30 mph	66	63
50 mph	72	67
70 mph	76	77

[1] Non-standard skidpad of 75-ft radius; see text.

CALCULATED DATA

	Chevrolet Camaro IROC-Z L98	Ford Mustang GT
Lb/bhp (test weight)	16.9	15.9
Bhp/liter	38.4	44.5
Mph/1000 rpm (top gear)	33.1	37.0
Engine revs @ 60 mph (top gear)	1810	1620

CUMULATIVE RATINGS—SUBJECTIVE EVALUATION

	Chevrolet Camaro IROC-Z L98	Ford Mustang GT	Comments
Performance:			
Engine	8.5	7.5	no substitute for cubic inches
Gearbox	6.0	7.5	a choice beats an automatic
Steering	7.5	8.5	Mustang is tighter on center
Brakes	8.0	7.0	a win for 4-wheel discs
Ride	6.5	7.5	Ford chose ride quality
Handling	8.5	7.0	Chevy chose handling ability
Body Structure	8.0	6.5	weight buys strength
Average	7.6	7.4	
Comfort/Controls:			
Driving position	9.0	7.5	Camaro is more sporting
Controls	8.0	8.0	two good but different approaches
Instrumentation	8.5	7.5	hurray for the 140-mph speedometer
Outward vision	6.5	6.0	neither one is best
Quietness	7.0	7.0	one is quiet, one sounds pretty
Heater/vent/air cond	9.0	9.0	two excellent systems
Ingress/egress	6.5	7.5	the taller car wins this one
Front seat	6.5	9.0	Ford's in all the right places
Rear seat	2.5	5.5	the Mustang's biggest advantage
Luggage & loading	6.0	5.5	both should be better
Average	7.0	7.3	
Design/Styling:			
Exterior styling	9.0	6.0	Chevy has this one right
Exterior finish	8.5	6.5	the best prototype wins
Interior styling	8.5	7.0	Ford's restyling doesn't do it
Interior finish	8.0	4.5	production cars may be better
Average	8.5	6.0	
Overall average	7.5	7.0	
Staff preferences:[1]			
Price independent	6	3	
Price dependent	5	4	

[1] With preferences, 1st choice = 2 points, 2nd choice = 1 point; three staff members involved.

FORD'S IMSA GTO
MUSTANG IS
PUSHING PORSCHE
TO THE LIMIT

Text and Photography
by Don Emmons

ROUSH RACER

Mention IMSA racing, and the image that immediately springs to mind is that of Porsche errors taking the checkered flag—time after time . . . after time. But as we noted in the December '86 issue of Mustang ("Mustang Probe"), the times are changing.

U.S. auto manufacturers have given notice to the Europeans that they've dominated the field long enough. From now on, American race cars are going to give American racing fans something to cheer about the next time they go to an IMSA race.

And Ford is leading the charge.

IMSA racing is divided into three classes: GTP, GTO, and GTU. The GTP class is for prototype machines, those all-out race cars that top out at 230 mph. These cars don't look anything like street machines, yet they're the stars of the IMSA/Camel GT Series. The GTO class is for cars with over-three-liter engines, and look much more like stock automobiles. Cars under three liters fall into the GTU class.

Ford is sponsoring two different programs in IMSA racing. The first includes a two-car GTP team which feature the radical Mustang Probes.

And in the GTO class, Ford is going all-out. There are two-to-four cars that are doing very well in this competition class. So well, in fact, that they took the GTO championship in 1985 and started off 1986 with some impressive showings.

The '86 season began with a fourth and fifth place overall in the 24-hour Daytona race behind three 962 Porsches. The 7/Eleven car piloted by Bruce Jenner and Scott Pruitt was fifth, which gave Ford a first and second place in the GTO class.

At the 12-hour Sebring race, Ford's banner was once again held high.

1. The shock absorber coil springs are interchangeable for various track conditions. Rear swaybar can be adjusted from the dash panel. AP racing disc brakes use 12-inch ventilated rotor.

2. Exhaust system is routed from headers over the right side of car and both sides exit here. This is mainly to keep heat away from driver's area.

3. Hatchback body allows access to the fuel cell and its plumbing. Forward bulkhead closes off driver's compartment from fuel tank.

4. Handle and knob at this side of dash panel allows driver to control adjustment of rear swaybar for fuel load and tire wear compensation. Brake proportioning valve adjusts the rear brake system.

5. A view from the passenger's side of the race car as it comes into Turn 9 at Riverside Raceway after going flat out down the long back straight. Bruce Jenner gave this writer a wild ride at full throttle.

6. The driver's side of dash panel looks clean and business-like. Rear side is really a maze.

RACER

Another fourth and fifth overall got Ford a first and second place in GTO class, and they were pushing the Porsche 962s again. The Jenner-Pruitt car captured fourth place.

The third endurance race was held at Riverside, California, a six-hour event. The Ford/GTO banner was riding on the single entry manned by Jenner and Pruitt. Their position was far back on the starting grid, but they moved up quickly, and ran first in class throughout most of the race, only to drop to second after a lengthy pit stop. They took second in GTO class and seventh overall.

This is where we caught up with the brightly painted Mustang piloted by Jenner and Pruitt. Ford hosted a press showing of their race cars a few days prior to race day, and I was able to take a few laps in the 7/Eleven

Mustang with Bruce Jenner at the wheel. It was a stimulating ride to say the least.

Roush Racing of Livonia, Michigan, is the team that builds and races the Mustangs and Capris that compete in IMSA and Trans-Am races—with the help of Ford's SVO Division, of course. Their two main drivers are Jenner and Pruitt. They co-drive in the long enduros, but compete separately in the short-distance events.

The Roush-built 7/Eleven Mustangs look basically like regular Mustang hatchbacks, but that's about as far as the similarity goes. The chassis is a specially constructed tube frame unit that is as state-of-the-art as any GTP, or, for that matter, any Indy race car. Yes, it's super-high-tech but still complies with the rules governing GTO race cars. They built the chassis of 1½-inch square mild steel with the rollcage and stress members constructed from 1½-inch round 4130 chromemoly tubing. Its wheelbase is the same as a stock Mustang's, as required by IMSA rules, but it is allowed a wider track due to the use of

wide racing wheels and tires.

Front suspension has unequal-length upper and lower control arms. Fabricated tubular A-arms and spindle are made in-house for these cars. Shocks at all four corners are Fox gas pressure coil-over units with a reserve canister to control the heat and performance of the shocks. They are adjustable for the shock and for the spring, thus allowing the driver to tailor the chassis to road conditions. Disc brakes are 12x1⅜-inches with AP four-part racing calipers.

A Ford 9-inch unit handles the rearend. The center section is a Winters cast aluminum unit. The Roush machine shop makes up the rest of the housing, down to the custom axles. The same size AP disc brakes are used at the rear. Fox coil-over shocks are used at the rear but the springs have a longer travel. Control for the rearend is by four trailing links with a Watts link.

The fully adjustable swaybar is a whopping 1⅜ inches. A ¾-inch unit is used at the rear along with an adjustable setup—so the rear can be

7. Three-inch rocker panel provides ground clearance and a low silhouette. The 16-inch BBS alloy rims use 25.5/12.5-16 Goodyear Eagles in front on 12-inch rims. Rear takes 14-inch rims with 27/14-16-inch rubber.

8. Car has to retain original top and windshield and doors must remain in stock position. Front and rear fender panels can be widened to cover tires. Body panels are fiberglass. Body weighs only 150 pounds. Race-ready, the car weighs in at 2600 pounds.

9. All suspension components were fabricated by the Roush Company. Tubular A-arms carry specially made spindles. Fox gas shocks use coil-over springs and a reservoir that mounts to frame member. Adjustable chrome swaybar is 1⅜ inches in diameter.

10. This Mustang race car definitely sits low to the ground. The 1½-inch flexible rubber extensions put the car as close to the racing surface as possible. Rules allow body width to be extended to cover wide racing tires.

11. Rear wing was cut down for '86 competition. IMSA felt that the larger unit gave the car an unfair advantage, but the '86 season has shown that it's not just the big tail that got them around the track so quickly.

12. Onboard air jacks make for quick pit stops. One of these large cylinders mounts to each corner of the chassis. Air supply comes from air hose connection mounted in quarter window.

RACER

changed as the car's weight changes due to fuel usage, or as tire wear changes the handling. A knob on the dash is turned to change the rear to compensate for those variations.

Power for this hard charger comes from the Roush engine department. Jack Roush takes a personal interest here. The basic unit is a 366-cubic-inch V8 using mostly SVO high-performance parts. The SVO block and alloy heads are used along with the SVO crankshaft and rods.

SVO manifolds were reworked some and a 780 Holley carburetor is used. Hand-built components include the exhaust system, heavy-duty radiator, and oil coolers. The transmission is a Wisemann 5-speed unit. All five ratios are independently changeable and spear gear combinations mean that gear changes can be made to fit the needs of a particular track. This and

the rearend ratios allow the team to set up the car for any track conditions.

Rules state that the vehicle must maintain a semblance to the stock model. The roof and windshield must remain stock and the doors have to be at the stock location. Other sheetmetal portions can be widened to fully cover the wide wheel/tire combination. Alterations have been made to the front end as a result of many hours of wind-tunnel testing to attain the best possible airflow. The trick wing on the rear was changed for '86 because the IMSA rules committee placed stronger restrictions on the Mustangs for this year. New rules cut the height of the wing 1½ inches and disallowed the end piece.

It was felt that the cars were just too competitive, which may well have been the case. The Roush Mustangs won nine of the 16 IMSA races and took first, second, and fifth in the points standings in '85. Those rule changes were supposed to cut the car's downforces, but after the first few events in '86 placed them fourth and fifth overall, behind the Porsche 962s,

it seems they were not hampered all that much.

As mentioned, the Roush team has two regular jockeys for their Mustangs. The first one is 1976 Olympic gold medalist in the decathlon, Bruce Jenner. He won his first car race in 1980 at the Long Beach Grand Prix and was bitten by the race bug. After a few rides in celebrity races, he got serious and went to driving school. He ran a limited schedule in 1985—seven races in the GTO Mustang—with very good results. He finished in the top five six times and wound up seventh in points standings.

For '86 he got the nod as full-time driver for the Roush team and is jockeying for points lead with teammate Scott Pruitt.

Twenty-six-year-old Scott Pruitt came on the Roush team mid-season last year and showed plenty of promise. He and Jenner have been smoking the tracks so far this year with outstanding showings in the long enduro races. Not bad for a Mustang GTO car with a couple of relative newcomers to the sport. *M*

13. Team drivers for the Ford Mustang GTO challenge are Bruce Jenner (right) and Scott Pruitt.

14. Six-liter V8 consists of mostly Ford SVO components. Engine uses a reworked SVO intake manifold and a single Holley 780 carburetor. Special heavy-duty radiator and coolers are used. Engine puts out over 600 horsepower.

15. Entire fiberglass front body panel can be removed, or—if desired for quick engine checks—only the hood can be removed. Body panels can be changed to make this one a Capri in just 25 minutes.

16. Main chassis was built from 1½-inch square tubing. Rollcage is the same size tubing but is round. Tires are limited to a maximum of 16 inches in width.

17. Dash panel houses more gauges than does a regular race car. These cars run nights during 24-hour enduro races so lights and other items are necessary. Moroso 12-grand tach is redlined at 8000. Small leather-rimmed steering wheel is by Momo.

Text and Photography
by Eric Rickman

SALEEN SOLUTION

GIVING AN EXTRA KICK TO SECON
AND THIRD-GENERATION PONIES

"**Y**ou get what you pay for," is an axiom that has stood the test of time. Detroit builds cars ranging from econo-boxes to limos, always within parameters that are a compromise between cost and desired product.

The Ford Motor Company has stretched this compromise pretty far toward the ideal end of the scale with their 5-liter GT Mustang. It is a lot of car for the money.

Steve Saleen of Saleen Autosport (Dept. HRM, 313 North Lake St., Burbank, CA 91502; 213/849-1017) has taken the additional step needed to "improve the breed" and make a real thoroughbred racer out of this little colt. Steve has not only succeeded in making the pony look better, but he's made it handle better too, yet kept it in a competitive price range with other stock GTs on the market.

Cosmetically, Steve has improved the little GT with the addition of a redesigned airdam up front, ground effects-type skirts at the sides, and a lower valance in the rear. A spoiler with the DOT-required "third eye" stop light has been added over the rear deck hatch. The use of Saleen color-coordinated graphics further enhance the car's overall appearance.

The use of shorter, heavier coil springs with "tailored" spring rates has lowered the car about 1½ inches despite the addition of the one-inch-larger 16x7-inch Riken "waffle" alloy wheels shod with General XP2000V-225/50 radial tires. Lowering the car serves to reduce the undercar air turbulence (i.e., drag).

All the aerodynamic trim is injection molded polyurethane, which is much more flexible than the commonly used fiberglass which tends to shatter on impact. Trim pieces are secured at the ends inside the wheelwells by sheetmetal screws and held to the body by 3M double-faced adhesive tape over their length—a unique but practical method that avoids butchering the body. The spoiler is bolted to the rear deck, as it generates a good deal of downforce at speed, enhancing the car's stability. All items are held to Ford's tolerances.

To improve the handling, Steve has installed Koni shocks and front struts re-valved to his specs to dampen the ride, in addition to the "designed rate" coil springs, resulting in true "sports car" ride and handling. Ford's 1.30-inch stabilizer bar is retained, with the substitution of Saleen graphite-impregnated urethane mounting bushings to free up the bar's action and absorb some of the running gear noise. Wheel alignment in high-speed cornering is retained by the use of a Koni upper tower control yoke. The use of the yoke, in addition to an engine compartment cross-brace, increased the car's cornering ability just over two seconds on a 20-second slalom course.

Right out of the gate this pony is

SALEEN

Color-coordinated graphics add a pleasing touch to the car's overall appearance. These are stepped blue tone panels on a white car. Ronal wheels are painted to match individual paint schemes.

pretty close to a thoroughbred in stock form. This is attested to by the fact that the California Highway Patrol uses this little runner as its designated freeway pursuit vehicle. With a *Motor Trend* magazine road test top speed of 139+mph and 0-to-60mph in 6.0 seconds, it would behoove you to think twice before trying to out-run it. As a quarter-horse, it covers the distance in 14.64 seconds, showing 92+mph at the finish line.

It is quite evident that the engine and drivetrain don't need any help. The 200hp H.O. engine in the Saleen Mustang is coupled to a 5-speed transmission in combination with Ford's 3.08:1 Traction Lok rearend to produce an almost ideal package. On special order you can get Ford's automatic overdrive transmission which features an electric clutch that locks up in high gear over 35 mph to eliminate transmission slippage. By not altering the engine or drivetrain, the Saleen retains Ford's EPA certification requirements and warranty program.

Ford approves of the Saleen Mustang to the extent that they have accepted Steve into their dealer's purchase program. Steve is only the second "privateer" to be thus honored. Carroll Shelby was the first. Remember him?

With Ford's acceptance, Steve is able to order cars built to his specifications. The Saleen is actually a stock Mustang on an LX chassis instead of the GT chassis, equipped with the aforementioned engine and drivetrain. Some GT hardware is included, such as the quick-ratio steering, sport seats, the GT instrument cluster upgraded with Saleen graphics and a 170mph speedo, and a left side "dead-pedal." Steve hasn't neglected the creature comforts while concentrating on performance, though. The cockpit is fancied up a bit with a Kenwood KRC-6000 sound system, a leather-wrapped Momo steering wheel, and a deluxe Escort radar warning receiver.

Being a road racer, it wasn't long before Steve realized he had a real winner in his stable, which prompted him to field a two-car racing team with General Tires sponsorship. The cars are entered in the SCCA Escort endurance stock class racing series. In the stock GT class, the Saleen runs against ZX Turbos, Pontiac Trans Ams, IROC Camaros, Mustang GTs, Mazdas, and Porsche 944s.

Steve's cars have won a 24-hour enduro after setting track records during qualifying and starting on the pole. This was the first win of its kind for Fords! The car has proven to be one of the quickest on the track, with the only competition coming from the 944 Porsches with their larger gas

Ronal IROC-style alloy wheels are another dress-up item. Clear Lexan headlight shields are available to improve aerodynamics. Shorter springs lower the car 1½ inches to reduce under-car air turbulence and drag.

With the addition of a rollcage and decals, your Saleen Mustang will be as race-ready as this one from Steve's two-car racing stable. His cars have set many qualifying records.

Ground effects trim not only looks good, but serves the useful purpose of smoothing airflow and shielding tire splash.

The use of Saleen Signature jewelry to replace the Mustang marques has been done very tastefully throughout the car.

Each car is serialized and registered with this signature plate. Numbers are stamped elsewhere on frame and body too. This is the first car produced in '85.

Saleen's lower rear valance reduces airstream updraft from under the car with accompanying dirt and moisture. Spoiler is bolted to rear deck to provide stabilizing downforce at speed.

The updated 170mph speedo is available separately, or as part of a complete Saleen Signature instrument cluster.

SALEEN

tanks and smaller engines. We're talking about 21.12-gallon tanks versus the Mustang's 15.4-gallon tank. Not to mention the Porsche engine, which at 2.5 liters is one-half the displacement of the Mustang engine, a four-banger against a V8. With equally matched machines, being able to eliminate a few pit stops in a 24-hour enduro adds up to a considerable lead.

Since the car is limited to stock trim, Steve is working on improving fuel economy to try and overcome the Porsche advantage.

Now for the good news! If you have a completely restored '73 or later Mustang, or new '85/'86 pony, just drop it off at Autosport (with some hay), and pick it up a few days later and you'll get a completely retrained Saleen thoroughbred, serialized and registered in Steve's stud book. Steve adds additional serial numbers to Ford's ID numbers and records them for later authentication of your car. You get a certified copy of your pony's bloodlines.

Clubs are already forming, and it looks like this bangtail will surely become a collectors' item. Limited production will ensure its scarcity in about 20 or 30 years. Certified registration will discourage unscrupulous parties from trying to create a phony pony Saleen from an early Mustang—a not-unheard-of practice in today's market.

If you can't spring for the $4000 to $5000 it takes to have Steve retrain your Mustang, all the parts and pieces are available to enable you to do it yourself. Kits are available for each stage of the conversion.

The cosmetic package has all the exterior trim parts, including wheels and tires, to improve both appearance and aerodynamics. The suspension package provides the springs, shocks, braces and bushings to make the car handle properly. Finally, there are the interior items: Kenwood 6000 radio and speakers, Momo steering wheel, sports seats, 170mph speedo, and Saleen instrument cluster, plus a much needed Escort radar detector.

The best part of this deal is the fact that you can buy the packages a piece at a time as your budget permits. D-I-Y cars will not be registered, however. Steve is committed to keeping all the items in stock for seven years to meet Ford's parts availability requirements.

If you have the hay, just contact your nearest Ford/Saleen dealer and ride one of these beauties right out of the stable for $14,000 to $16,000. Compare these prices against other GT cars—IROC Camaros, ZX Turbos, not to mention Porsches—that go for a *bit* more. Plug these numbers into your dollar vs. performance/pleasure formula and you will see that it is the best ride for the money. *M*

Front strut, spring and stabilizer mounting bushing (arrow) have been replaced. A simple job with a pair of jacks, one under the body, the other to raise and lower the A-arm.

Rear suspension mods are another straightforward parts-swapping job. Koni shocks are re-valved to Saleen specs to tailor the handling. Horizontal shock prevents wheelhop.

This is only half-a-lot of cars already sold, with a waiting list backlogged. Steve's production is limited by his allotment from Ford. Starting with 50 in '84, and just over 200 in '85, his target is 1000 per year. Still limited production.

Basic suspension mods consist of replacing springs, struts and shocks. "Designed rate" springs are shorter and heavier than stock. This is a set for one side, front right, rear left.

Die-molded polyurethane pieces are used to improve aerodynamics. Riken 16x7 "waffle" wheels are mounted with General 225VR50 HP radial tires. Other combinations are available.

A Momo leather-wrapped steering wheel adds a luxurious touch to the interior. Note easy access to instrument cluster which can be swapped for a complete Saleen Signature assembly.

Installation is simplified by Saleen's use of 3M double-faced adhesive tape to secure aerodynamic trim. Sheetmetal screws are used only at the ends within the wheelwells.

Autosport is able to turn out two-to-three cars per day in this small area of the Saleen shop. Production will increase as Ford's allotment increases. Parts swapping and installation is relatively easy for the do-it-yourself builder.

REVIEW MUSTANG GT

For those who remember the Boss 302, the pony gallops again.

BY MEL NICHOLS

Lancaster, California—It was the way the tail slid; the way it stayed flat and clean and sent its message back; the way it said, "Give me some opposite lock now, and perhaps a little more power." It was the way the 1987 Mustang GT romped around the track, demonstrating that it had balance and flair as well as performance, that sent my spirits soaring. Here, after almost two decades in the wilderness, was a Mustang that could be *driven.* And, as good as it felt on the track during those few quick tryout laps, it was the notion of peeling away from Willow Springs and running hard through the hills that really had my palms itching.

I'd come to the new 5.0 GT skeptically. When Mustang was a name wreathed in glory, I knew the Boss 302 well, and I had enjoyed my share of Shelbys. But it was just about all downhill from there, with the once proud name of America's favorite pony car touted ignominiously through the '70s by the horrendous Mustang II. There was some improvement with the launch of the current series in 1979, but the climb back didn't really get cracking until Mike Kranefuss transferred from running Ford's European racing program to start up Dearborn's Special Vehicle Operations in late 1980. First fruit was the '84 model Mustang SVO. What mattered wasn't so much the 205 horsepower that wizards like Jack

Roush, working to Kranefuss's brief, duly wrung from the SVO's 2.3-liter turbo engine; it was the work on the suspension. Showroom confusion (why would buyers want to pay more for a 2.3-liter turbo when they could have a 5.0-liter V-8 packing almost identical power?) led to the demise this year of the Mustang SVO in favor of the V-8–powered GT.

But the SVO did not come and go in vain. Its ability and appeal as a modern Mustang that spoke loudly to drivers showed everyone at Ford, from chairman Donald Petersen down, how good this aging coupe could be. That fit with Ford's efforts to revitalize its corporate image, and the wheels were put into motion to transfer the prowess of the SVO Mustang to the GT.

The familiar 5.0-liter (302 cubic inch) V-8 had been getting steadily stronger since it rejoined the Mustang with just 157 bhp in 1982. Last year it was up to 200 bhp. New cylinder heads and induction improvements lift the '87 model's output to a healthy 225 bhp at 4200 rpm—matching the power of the 5.7-liter Camaro IROC-Z—with a neat 300 pounds-feet of torque at 3200 rpm. The standard transmission has gone from a four- to a five-speed manual, with an optional four-speed automatic replacing the old three-speed. This lusty drivetrain goes into an almost fifteen-foot

PHOTOGRAPHY BY TIM WREN

MUSTANG GT

car with a curb weight of 3160 pounds, setting the scene for performance aplenty.

The best news is that the Mustang GT, thanks to the inspiration of the Mustang SVO, has a suspension that enables this performance to be put to proper use. At the front, caster changes reduce camber loss in the corners, and the car uses the old SVO Mustang's plastic ball joints, retuned bushings, and better mounts for the anti-roll bar. Modified MacPherson struts have the springs mounted separately on the lower arms, and the damper inserts are gas-pressurized. The Special Vehicle Operations development of a new crossmember also allowed different front suspension pickup points, which in turn permit the fitting of decently large P225/60VR-15 Goodyear gatorbacks running 35 psi for reduced rolling resistance.

The Mustang still has its live rear axle, but the unit has been strengthened, had its bushes retuned, and is tied down pretty well by the four links locating it and the four gas-filled shock absorbers. An anti-roll bar helps, too. The disappointment is that, where the Mustang SVO had

disc brakes all around, the GT's 10.9-inch front discs are backed up merely by 9.0-inch rear drums. The steering, however, is honest-to-goodness rack-and-pinion; 2.2 turns lock to lock make it quick, and power assistance makes it manageable.

Not only does this year's Mustang perform a lot better than its predecessors, it also looks a lot better, even if its coefficient of drag is still a pretty staid 0.38. Although the body has been in production for eight years, the GT's revamp links it reasonably well to the smooth aero look Ford now presents so successfully with the Taurus, the Thunderbird

Turbo Coupe, and the Mercury Sable. The nasal treatment, with the flush headlights and combined spoiler and underbumper air scoop, imparts an impression of performance without going too far. The additions to the sills don't get out of hand, either, and the rear spoiler is a paragon of taste compared with the XR4Ti's— or even the Mustang SVO's. The louvered taillight treatment is the thing most likely to draw adverse comment. Overall, the GT looks like it means business, yet stays pretty enough, without having the same sort of gut-wrenching beauty as the Camaro or the Corvette.

The quality of the interior redesign is even more impressive—a fine blend of tastefulness and function. It's no accident that it seems more European than American: it was designed by Trevor Creed, who had a telling hand in the Merkur interior, among many other notable works, before transferring from Ford of Europe (and recently moving to Chrysler). What you find in the GT's cockpit is a well-positioned wheel and a beautifully clear instrument panel. The latter is edged by twin pods holding the minor controls, with

clear and simple knobs for air conditioning and ventilation high enough on the center console section to be seen and reached easily. The way the facia recedes in front of the passenger creates a feeling of airiness. There's nothing pretentious or awkward anywhere. You find, too, that the driver's seat is as comfortable as it looks (with electric lumbar adjustment, a nice touch). Best of all, however, is the discovery that the brake and throttle pedals are arranged for perfect heel and toe gearshifting.

The message is clear. Ford has begun to acknowledge the priorities of driving. The contrast with a straight-line monster like the Buick Regal Grand National, where even the tachometer doesn't rise above joke status, could not be starker.

At Willow Springs, the Mustang GT was part of the American team doing battle with the Holden Calais Director from Australia for the story elsewhere in this issue. Here we soon learned, happily, that the Mustang was ready to deliver the performance and no-nonsense drivability it promised. Observed clockings (at Willow Springs's half-mile elevation) of 15.1 seconds in the standing quar-

ter-mile and 0 to 60 mph in 7.1 seconds were one indication, and the midrange response of the injected V-8 was another. But the way the Mustang's handling turned out to be so predictable and progressive, so effortless and enjoyable, was the message from Mecca. The car turned into the bends cleanly, with understeer never passing the point of pleasing stability, then nudged through a long period of neutrality into progressive oversteer, talking all the way. A nudge of opposite lock held the tail. A touch more power pushed it out farther, with a little more lock balancing that, too. From the outset, the Mustang felt like a car that could be driven fast and safely and satisfyingly. It had all the right sporting attributes, yet there was also something quite nice about its character. It came down to one word: forgiving.

When it was all over with the other cars at Willow Springs, photographer Tim Wren and I took off, suitably enthused, and headed deep into the Sierra Nevada. We found perfect roads: roads that weaved through canyons and then climbed high to run around mountainsides before

diving back down again. These roads also ran straight enough, every now and then, for the Mustang to be pressed hard in fourth with its speedo needle starting to go around the clock for the second time and the genuine speed climbing upwards of 130 mph, with more in hand.

For all its power and performance—and we knew the acceleration figures would have been better nearer to sea level—the Mustang felt so manageable; it was exciting, yet handy, rather than wild and headstrong. Its size helped. After some of the Mustang's early ancestors and the Camaro (almost fourteen inches longer and four inches wider), the GT seemed small and nimble. Even on the narrow stretches and where the bends were visibly off-camber, there was nothing intimidating about driving it hard and fast.

Unleashing the V-8 brought clean power from low revs, with gear changes at the 4800 rpm "orange-line" on the tachometer ideal for rocketing down the straights and between the bends. Here the Mustang showed the age-old advantage of its large, multicylinder engine: lusty performance from almost any revs. It

THE CONVERTIBLE GT
Open-air motoring adds greatly to the 5.0-liter Mustang's virtues—and vice versa.

The sun was dropping and the mist was closing in, but I left the top down anyway. And as the Mustang nipped along the valley taking me back out of the Sierra Nevada, I began to experience one of those priceless drives that can only be had in a convertible.

I knew the car was fast—I'd been driving its coupe sister for two days, and while the convertible weighed 134 pounds more and suffered poorer aerodynamics, it didn't give much away in acceleration. More noticeable was a drop in the roadholding and handling, probably caused by reduced body shell rigidity, which showed itself through scuttle shake over bumps and judders when the doors were opened and shut. It seemed par for the course among coupe-derived convertibles, but it was some distance from the build quality of the Mustang GT.

Still, the grip remained on the upper side of strong, and the handling stayed predictable and sporting. The performance flowing from the 5.0-liter V-8 allowed the Mustang convertible a punchy character that has been lamentably missing from far too many open cars of the past two decades. Yet, thanks to the seat and the ride, comfort was kept in the mix. So as I dashed down from the mountains, I enjoyed the sort of verve that had been so pleasing in the GT, with the extra dimension of having nothing but my hat over my head.

As it happened, the evening's changing weather would make this an experience to remember. Above the white mist collecting near the ground, the sun's last rays sprayed the hillsides golden, and above them spread a perfectly azure sky. Then, in the flat country, the mist grew deep and gray and cold. The driving grew lonely and eerie, and I tugged my hat down and tightened my scarf and turned up the heater, reveling in this involvement with the elements. From behind came the burble of the V-8's lusty exhaust, a better accompaniment than any radio.

When the mist cleared, I let the Mustang run to somewhere around 100 mph, and learned that the airflow was still smooth enough over the windshield for there to be no buffeting or discomfort. The car sang for 100 miles of this fast and perfect motoring, then joined the throng heading into Los Angeles. The cold, the solitude, and the smell of farms and fields and trees were replaced by the wafting warmth of the coast, the hiss of a thousand tires, and the sweet smell of hot oil.

In a filling station, I asked the student who was firing off questions faster than he was putting fuel into the Mustang's tank if this was a car for him. "Are you kidding?" he yelled. "I'd *kill* for one of these!" I thought back over the drive I'd just enjoyed, and about the way the new Mustang blends the best virtues of a convertible with such intoxicating performance for a price of $15,852, and how that combination overshadows the fiddliness of tugging the boot over the folded roof and the low-rent sound of the doors shutting. The fact is, the Mustang comes closer to being irresistible than any convertible this side of a Corvette or a Mercedes SL. —MN

TIM WREN

MUSTANG GT

was nicest in the midrange, however, responding with real grunt and a lovely burble that came bouncing back off the canyon walls.

The smooth sections of road showed the car off best. It was glorious to come fast at the bends, brake hard, and go down through the gears—an action made pleasing by that easy heel and toe facility—and then to crank on the power from 2500 rpm or so and wind the engine out, with the car straightening up and streaming powerfully away from the apex. It was classic sports stuff, the sort of driving experience you long to go on enjoying.

So much of the Mustang seemed so right. The clutch was light enough to go unnoticed. The shift was a trifle notchy but worked pleasingly, as long as you remembered that the first-second and third-fourth legs in the gate were closer than the movement over to fifth and back. One or two missed selections, from second to fifth and vice versa, were enough to implant a little caution. Second gear emerged as the high point, run-

ning to around 65 mph before the engine started asking for third, and delivering exhilarating punch.

The steering stayed pleasant all the time—quick, smooth, and precise, with the right sort of feel. When the wheels encountered slippery patches, the message came through to the hands loud and clear, just as it did from the tail to the seat of the pants. That emerged as one of the Mustang's most endearing characteristics: the communicative nature of its suspension. This was important. Gravel strewn across the entrances to several bends showed how easily the otherwise prodigious grip of the wide tires could be broken in a

trice—at the front if you were going too fast, or at the rear if you applied too much power. The inference was that the Mustang, like most of its high-powered contemporaries, would need real care on ice and snow. But at least there was the knowledge that it had the response and the handling to stay on the happy side of decent.

As we stormed up and down the mountains, bumpy sections showed that the suspension was good but far from perfect. The nose weaved noticeably under heavy braking into the bends when the approach was rippled, and at times the tail danced as the weight transferred a bit too much to the front. It never got out of hand, but it called for concentration and the readiness to tweak on a swift flick of countering lock. It was important to ensure that the braking was pretty much over and done with before turning into the bend. Wait too long, and the result was one of two things: the tail snapping out or, worse, the front brakes locking up and the nose sliding straight on. But it was a precaution easily maintained, and what it revealed was the absence of ideal quality from a chassis that otherwise displayed good handling characteristics. But then, how much can be done with a live axle in a road car where ride smoothness must also be a priority?

Within its own compromise, the Mustang demonstrated satisfactory ride comfort. Even on roads that were punishing by American standards, it never deteriorated to the point of crashing or jarring. There was nothing to make you think you wouldn't like to drive many hundreds of miles. Nor were there creaks and groans from the body or trim. We had one of the switches pop out of its pod on the binnacle, but for the rest, the Mustang emerged with creditable build quality.

Of course, it has a fair amount of practicality as well. Although there is no headroom to spare, adults can sit in the back, and with the hatchback there is the convenience of folding the split rear seats to lengthen the shallow luggage space.

From the mountains, we went down to the desert again and learned that at well above 130 the Mustang maintained good directional stability and never became too noisy. It had a completeness to go with its sportiness, and a level of refinement to go with its performance that was missing from the great but rugged old Mustangs of two decades ago.

Drifting along with the traffic after two days of driving, it began to occur to me that, as the Mustang name goes into its twenty-fourth year, the 1987 GT is probably the best of the breed. Its acceleration is in the league of the classic and very low-geared Boss 302 (standing quarter-mile in 14.6 seconds, 0 to 60 mph in 6.0 seconds), yet it's considerably faster (Ford quotes 145 mph, against a recorded 118 mph for the Boss 302). Feed in the fact that the handling is equally good and the level of refinement is in another sphere, and you have a Mustang that stands above even its most distinguished predecessors. Like them, it isn't perfect, but it's darn good. I liked Tim Wren's comment after hours at the wheel, driving hard. "It doesn't have the grace and refinement of a good European car this fast," he said, and started to grin. "But at the end of the day you have to say, 'Damn—that was fun!'"

FORD MUSTANG GT

GENERAL:
Front-engine, rear-wheel-drive coupe
2 + 2-passenger, 2-door steel body
Base price/price as tested $12,106/$14,145

MAJOR EQUIPMENT:
Air conditioning $788
Sunroof $355
AM/FM/cassette $523
Leather interior (convertible only) $415
Cruise control $176

ENGINE:
OHV V-8, iron block and heads
Bore x stroke 4.0 x 3.0 in (101.6 x 76.2mm)
Displacement 302 cu in (4942cc)
Compression ratio 9.2:1
Fuel system electronic multiport injection
Power SAE net 225 bhp @ 4200 rpm
Torque SAE net 300 lb-ft @ 3200 rpm
Redline 6000 rpm

DRIVETRAIN:
5-speed manual transmission
Gear ratios (I) 3.35 (II) 1.93 (III) 1.29 (IV) 1.00 (V) 0.68
Final-drive ratio 2.73:1

MEASUREMENTS:
Wheelbase 100.5 in
Track front/rear 56.6/57.0 in
Length 179.3 in
Width 69.1 in
Height 52.1 in
Curb weight 3160 lb
Weight distribution front/rear 59/41%
Fuel capacity 15.4 gal

SUSPENSION:
Independent front, with MacPherson struts, lower control arms, coil springs, anti-roll bar
Live-axle rear, with unequal-length upper and lower control arms, coil springs, anti-roll bar

STEERING:
Rack-and-pinion, variable power-assisted

BRAKES:
10.1-in vented discs front
9.0-in drums rear

WHEELS and TIRES:
15 x 7.0-in cast aluminum wheels
225/60VR-15 Goodyear Eagle VR tires

PERFORMANCE (manufacturer's estimated data):
0–60 mph in 6.1 sec
Standing ¼-mile in 14.4 sec @ 96 mph
Top speed 145 mph
EPA city driving 16 mpg

MAINTENANCE:
Headlamp unit $41.67
Front quarter-panel $73.00
Brake pads front wheels $17.00
Air filter $11.40
Oil filter $4.50
Recommended oil change interval 7500 miles

	EXCELLENT	GOOD	FAIR	POOR
ENGINE				
power				●
response				●
smoothness			●	
DRIVETRAIN				
shift action		●		
power delivery			●	
STEERING				
effort				●
response				●
feel				●
RIDE				
general comfort			●	
roll control				●
pitch control				●
HANDLING				
directional stability				●
predictability				●
maneuverability				●
BRAKES				
response			●	
modulation			●	
effectiveness			●	
GENERAL				
ergonomics				●
instrumentation			●	
roominess		●		
seating comfort			●	
fit and finish			●	
storage space		●		
OVERALL				
dollar value				●
fun to drive				●

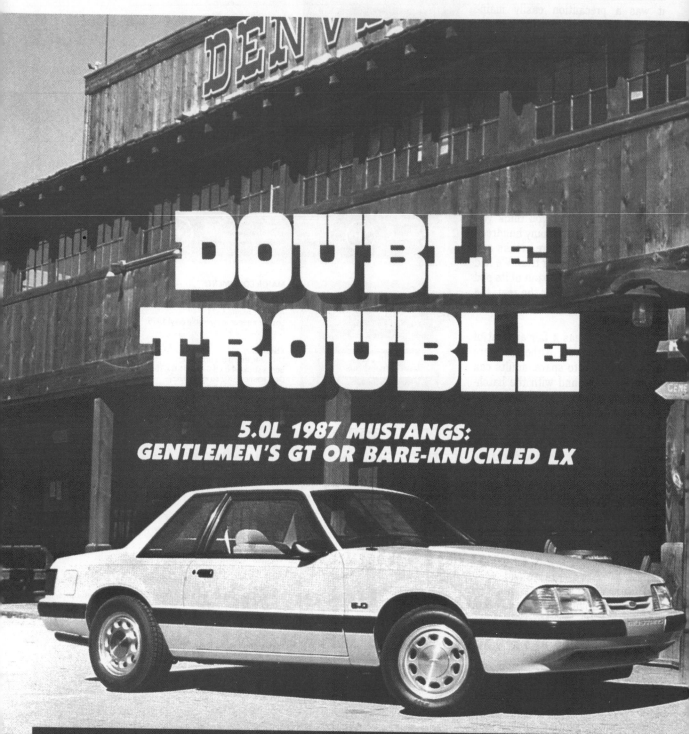

DOUBLE TROUBLE

5.0L 1987 MUSTANGS:
GENTLEMEN'S GT OR BARE-KNUCKLED LX

By John Baechtel

The '82 Mustang GT will surely be remembered as the car that launched the second golden age of musclecars. It was the first of the new breed of performance cars to show some real speed, and Ford engineers have steadily refined it into one of the most capable performance sedans available. In an era when most automakers are proud to have their top performance car running in the 14's, Ford has two distinctly different Mustangs capable of performing this feat—while matching more expensive performers corner for corner. Mustang's credentials are worth the price of admission at nearly any performance arena, and Ford continues to fortify its position as a performance leader by developing the car to its maximum potential.

The GT is the headliner in this performance duet, but the LX model steals the show if you're going strictly by the numbers. By virtue of its lighter weight (approximately 300 pounds), the LX emerges as the 0-to-60 and quarter-mile sprint king, lacking only a bit more traction to make it a true 13-second factory piece capable of running 0 to 60 in under 6 seconds. Bolt on a pair of slicks and the Mustang LX is a guaranteed 13-second street fighter.

LX models can be ordered as hatchbacks or sedans, either looking as docile as the day is long—until you spy the 5.0L emblems and the fat rubber under the fenders. Without air conditioning, the LX is a real lightweight that qualifies as the best street sleeper you can buy today. It carries the same underpinnings as the GT, thereby matching

GT ENGINE

GT INTERIOR

GT TURBINE WHEEL

its more sophisticated brother in cornering and handling capacity. Both cars are offered with the 5-speed manual overdrive transmission or a 4-speed automatic with overdrive.

The GT's strong suit is its smart new appearance, thanks to aero refinements that follow Ford's current aerodynamic trend. To some extent the LX also benefits from this treatment, but the GT is boldly enhanced with new air dams, side skirts, and a new rear wing. The GT gets newly styled "Turbine Wheels," while the LX is equipped with the snappy styled aluminum wheels that formerly graced GT models.

The LX interior is functional and comfortable. The absence of electric windows and door locks isn't annoying; but the unfinished-looking, two-tone dash treatment is, depending on color combination. In contrast, the GT inte-

rior is fully upholstered and richly finished with all the amenities desirable in a true GT-class car.

Both cars have the 5.0L H.O. engine with new modifications to enhance power for 1987. The tuned runner sequential port fuel-injection system has revised intake runners for higher flow and a new 60mm throttle body rated at 622-cfm, replacing last year's 58mm, 541-cfm unit. Standard 5.0L injectors deliver 14 pounds of fuel per hour, while the H.O. engine is fitted with injectors that deliver 19 pounds per hour. The standard 5.0L passsenger car cylinder head (E6SE-6049-AA) has been replaced with a higher-flowing truck cylinder head (E5TE-6049-AB), and the compression ratio has been reduced from 9.2:1 to 9.0:1. The 1986 engine used a forged, flat-top piston, while the 1987 version features a forging with a

.030-inch dish.

The cylinder block is a carryover from 1986, when cylinder wall and deck thicknesses were increased and the bores were siamesed to ensure perfectly round cylinders. The block

LX ENGINE

LX INTERIOR

Spec Sheet	1987 Mustang GT	1987 Mustang LX
RETAIL:		
Base Price	$12,106	$8271
Price as Tested	$14,158	$10,581
ENGINE:		
Type	OHV 90-degree V8	OHV 90-degree V8
Bore & Stroke	4.00 x 3.00-inch 101.6 x 76.2mm	4.00 x 3.00-inch 101.6 x 76.2mm
Displacement	302-cid, 5.0L	302-cid, 5.0L
Compression Ratio	9.0:1	9.0:1
Bhp @ rpm	225 @ 4400, MT 220 @ 4000, AT	225 @ 4400, MT 220 @ 4000, AT
Torque @ rpm	300 @ 3000	300 @ 3000
Induction System	Sequential Port Fuel-injection	Sequential Port Fuel-injection
DRIVETRAIN:		
Transmission	5-speed manual with overdrive	5-speed manual with overdrive
Axle Ratio	2.73:1	3.08:1
CHASSIS:		
Front Suspension	Nitrogen-filled gas struts, 1.3-inch stabilizer bar	Nitrogen-filled gas struts, 1.3-inch stabilizer bar
Rear Suspension	4-bar link with coil springs, gas shocks with horizontal axle damper and .82-inch stabilizer bar	4-bar link with coil springs, gas shocks with horizontal axle damper and .82-inch stabilizer bar
Steering Ratio	15:1	15:1
Brakes	Front: 11-inch vented discs Rear: 9 x 1.73-inch drums	Front: 11-inch vented discs Rear: 9 x 1.73-inch drums
Wheels	15 x 7 Turbine Wheel	15 x 7 styled aluminum
Tires	P225/60VR15 Goodyear Gatorbacks	P225/60VR15 Goodyear Gatorbacks
GENERAL:		
Curb Weight	3351 pounds	3046 pounds
Wheelbase	100.5 inches	100.5 inches
Fuel Capacity	15.4 gallons	15.4 gallons
PERFORMANCE:		
Quarter-mile	14.60 @ 96	14.17 @ 99
Power-to-weight	14.88 lbs./hp	13.09 lbs./hp
0-60 mph	6.3 seconds	6.1 seconds
Skidpad	.83g	.83g

weighs 126 pounds with the added material.

Ford's tubular exhaust headers were revised to achieve commonality with the engine as installed in a Mark VII LSC Lincoln. This required minor re-shaping of the tubes. The new part numbers are E6ZE-9428-BA (left hand) and E6ZE-9429-BA (right hand). Both the GT and the LX are equipped with the 2.25-inch dual exhaust system with dual catalysts and H-pipe.

Major suspension changes include increased travel on the front struts and 11-inch vented brake discs. Earlier models were fitted with 10-inch front disc brakes.

Both cars handle similarly, but the lighter LX exhibits better balance due to some 300 pounds less weight. The LX is the real nightstalker, but the GT is still the ticket if you're into high-visibility profilin'. In either case, the 1987 Mustang GT and Mustang LX still retain their "best buy" status for performance car shoppers. **HR**

At best, it was anti-climactic as the curtain drew back to reveal the '87 Ford Mustang GT. The gathered national and international automotive journalists took just a tiny pause from their polite conversation, not exactly an auspicious welcome for a new edition of America's pony-car. Indeed, even in its revamped '87 form, the Mustang's current external design is getting a little long in the tooth. But put yourself in Ford's shoes.

In 1965, Ford introduced what was to become the hottest-selling new model in automotive history. Every other manufacturer was knocked silly as the Mustang packed Ford dealer showrooms with new-car buyers while the others were left clamoring to catch up. By 1968, Chevrolet had introduced the Camaro, Chrysler the Barracuda, American Motors the Javelin, and Pontiac the Firebird. Ford's two-year head start was clearly dwindling.

Much to the delight of its new competitors, and to the dismay of Mustang fans, Ford's misguided designers, uninformed as to the Mustang's image, much less its market, took to heavy-handed sweeping design changes that, by the mid-'70s, had

1987 Ford Mustang GT
New blood for Ford's proud pony
by Rick Titus

PHOTOGRAPHY BY BOB D'OLIVO

turned America's pony-car sweetheart into a mid-Atlantic gunboat. Overweight, underfed, and looking like a cast-off from Thunderbird crash testing, the Mustang made a radical change in design and concept direction when Ford moved to reintroduce the model under the Mustang II tag. Based largely on the Pinto platform, the Mustang II was closer to the original Mustang roots, but, dreadfully underpowered, missed the mark as a real pony-car, a market segment that Camaro and Firebird had come to own.

Finally, in 1978, the Mustang came right, and General Motors salesmen started to hear the word Ford in their showrooms again as would-be F-body buyers suddenly had a product for

For what is surely an aging design, it looks the best it has to date

comparison. The Mustang was back with a V-8, and to prove it, automotive magazines started doing Camaro versus Mustang comparos again. The once smog-choked limp-wristed pony-cars started leading the return to real performance cars. In that vein, Ford was quickest to respond, with rapid suspension improvements and a strong small-block 302-cu-in. engine that flat outran the Camaro's 305 motor. The Chevy still remained strong on overall handling, and its brakes paled the Mustang's. Yet, Mustang sales figures improved, and, for Ford, all seemed right in the world again.

Given the Mustang's disaster in the '70s and recovery in the '80s, it's easy to understand why Ford has been reluctant to alter the Mustang's appearance. Facelifts and continued engine and suspension improvements have become the norm as annual updates.

For 1987, the trend to facelifts and once-over improvements continues. There is, however, more good news this year than there has been in the past. First, the exterior. For what is surely an aging design, it looks the best it has to date. An aerodynamically cleaner nosepiece is highlighted by flush-fitting headlamps and new lower lip inlet duct. A new, flush-mounted rear-quarter window gives the Mustang an uncluttered look. The impression of a lower beltline is enhanced by the redesigned body side skirt and rubstrip package. The air inlet vents on the lower leading edge of each fender well are functional, but Ford chose not to follow through and effectively guide the inlet air for brake cooling or any other aerodynamic assistance. The round, front-spoiler-placed driving lamps stand out as a tad odd, but the overall look is much meaner.

The "ground-effects" skirting package runs around the tail of the Mustang, giving the car a much lower rear end appearance. A rather dramatic rear wing comes as stock on the GT model, and directs air to the benefit of the overall high-speed handling of the GT. But as good as all this tail-end treatment is, it's marred by the 1950s taillight design. It's the kind of stuff "Big Daddy" Roth would just eat up. Molded as one piece, the lou-

vered look is painted body color, making the darker-color cars less subject to the ill effects of the lamps' appearance.

From a performance standpoint, the '87 Mustang GT sees several useful improvements. The current 200-hp engine, introduced in 1982 with 4-bbl carburetor induction system, is now fuel-injected, an '86 upgrade, and sports-modified cylinder head bumps the power to around 230 hp. The changes seem to help the overall driveability of the powerplant as well.

Ford made a sizeable effort for 1987 to improve the sound deadening in the Mustang platform. Corrugated firewall panels and sound-deadening adhesives give the '87 Mustang a rock-solid feel. It is, in fact, one of the first things you notice when you close the door. Road noise and engine vibration are cut nearly in half, and, yet, you still get the benefit of the race-bred Ford small-block, as the Mustang's exhaust note puts that certain little magic in the air.

The Mustang's major weakness, more in terms of Showroom Stock competition than any street use, is its brakes. Ford designers chose to enlarge the front vented discs, but continued to use leftover Pinto drums on the rear. This proves all the more annoying since Ford installed the rear disc brake package on the turbocharged SVO 4-cylinder Mustang that is now defunct. It seems the rear disc brakes died with it. This is appalling, considering that Ford flies the tall flag of performance over the Mustang, yet doles its best brakes out to whiney little four-bangers and their luxo lines.

Inside the GT, Ford has an all-new instrument and dash panel. Side window de-fog vents, full shut-off A/C

Road noise and engine vibrations are cut nearly in half, yet, you still get the benefit of the race-bred small block

vents, pod-mounted switches and smooth semi-gloss texture present a more current look. Frankly, the instrument pod smacks of Japan, but it does place the headlamp, emergency flashers, rear window defroster, and fog lamp controls right at hand. The gauge package is fairly conventional, with fuel, water temp, oil pressure, and charge instruments as standard on the GT.

New door and quarter-panel trim

gets uprated fabrics, and the armrests are slightly longer than last year's, lending better support. New seat designs include power lumbar support, concealed thigh-support handle, and new fabrics, as well. The whole interior feels better, and, combined with the new efforts toward noise control, the '87 Mustang has a greatly elevated feel of quality.

After several key Ford Motor Company executives gave the entire Ford 1987 lineup pitch, we were invited outside to give the new products a whirl. It proved interesting, however, that the first two cars driven out of the parking lot, where Ford had lined up 16 of its '87 products, were the only two Mustang GTs Ford brought. Seems for all the sameness, this is still the hottest car in the line. 'Nuff said. [Mt]

TECH DATA

1987 Mustang GT

POWERTRAIN
Vehicle configuration	Front engine, rear drive
Engine configuration	V-8, OHV, 2 valves/cylinder
Displacement	5000 cc (302.0 cu in.)
Max. power (SAE net)	225 hp @ 4200 rpm
Max. torque (SAE net)	300 lb-ft @ 3200 rpm
Transmission	5-sp. man.
Final drive ratio	1.85:1

CHASSIS
Suspension, f/r	Independent/live axle
Brakes, f/r	Disc/drum
Steering	Rack and pinion, power assist
Wheels	15 x 7.0 in., cast alloy
Tires	P225/60VR15

DIMENSIONS
Wheelbase	2552 mm (100.5 in.)
Overall length	4554 mm (179.3 in.)
Curb weight	1261 kg (2782 lb)
Fuel capacity	58.2 L (15.4 gal)

PERFORMANCE
Acceleration, 0-60	6.20 sec
Standing quarter mile	14.99 sec/93.9 mph
Braking, 60-0	144 ft
Lateral acceleration	0.84 g

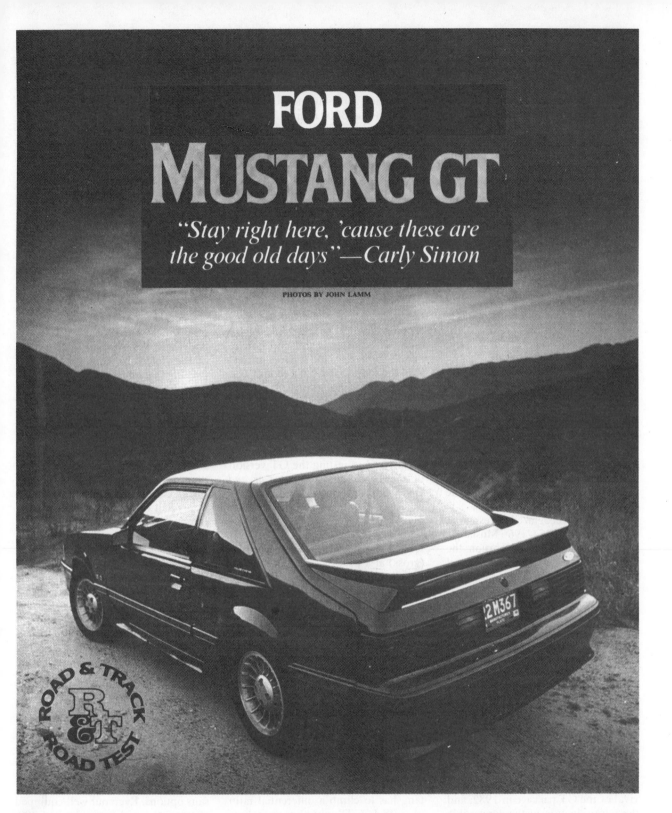

FORD
MUSTANG GT

"Stay right here, 'cause these are the good old days"—Carly Simon

PHOTOS BY JOHN LAMM

ROAD & TRACK
R&T
ROAD TEST

L EGENDS EXPAND WITH time. Fish grow larger, warriors mightier, women more pulchritudinous. Automotive legends are no different; in fact nothing in the universe grows faster and sleeker with the passage of time than the cars we lusted for in our youth.

For those who did their lusting in the Sixties, few cars are remembered more fondly than the original Ford Mustang—the One, True Youthmobile and progenitor of all ponycars. For those who remember, Ford's present pony must seem a bit lame. It is, after all, nought but a shortened Fairmont, motivated by what little V-8 has been left to us by two Middle Eastern oil embargoes and a final, grudging admission that automobile exhaust is, well, poisonous. Certainly, today's technology has endowed it with sophistication unheard of in those days of fond memory. But how can it compare to the kicking, snorting maverick (sorry) that first set our hearts ablaze so many years ago?

How indeed. Casting sentiment aside, a strong case can be made that the current Mustang GT is the best of the breed, the Mustang that has finally grown into the Mustang legend.

Return with me now, to the summer of 1964. The Ford Mustang, by most accounts the most successful new car *ever*, had already graced the covers of *Time* and *Newsweek*, with proud papa Lee Iacocca beaming by its side. But somewhere off the beaten path of mainstream journalism, the automotive enthusiast press had turned its collective thumb downward. In its August issue, *Road & Track* waxed ambivalent over the Mustang's styling, harshly criticized its ergonomics and shrank in horror from its "frankly sloppy suspension." The editors suggested that, were it possible to drive the car blindfolded, the Mustang "would be indistinguishable from any of half a dozen other Detroit compacts," and concluded that Ford had "simply built all the familiar characteristics for which the typical American sedan has been cursed so long, into a sporty looking package."

Right-coast writers liked it no better. *Automobile Quarterly* founder L. Scott Bailey invested in one for Nuccio Bertone to rebody, just to prove that the Italians could have done a better job. Even the first Mustang GTs that appeared that September failed to impress; the editors of *Car and Driver* cited the GT's lack of refinement and expressed a strong preference for the Plymouth Barracuda Formula S.

It seems we recognized the essential *rightness* of the 1964–1966 Mustang's shape, the allure of its proportion, the perfect appropriateness of its detail only later, as subsequent Mustangs swelled and bloated into facelessness. Then the first fuel crisis brought the Pinto-based Mustang II, about which the less is said, the better. The Mustang we thought we had loved was gone, martyred by the environmentalists, the insurance companies, the OPEC cartel. By the time a healthy, vital Mustang reappeared in 1979, it already was hopelessly overshadowed by its now-"classic" ancestor.

But the Ford Motor Co, like any other automaker, is in business to sell cars, not history. Dearborn groomed its new Mustang with a promising revival of the GT package in 1982, and the reintroduction of the convertible version the following year. Horsepower ratings edged ever higher, from 157 to 175 to 205 and most recently to 225 bhp. Ford also treated the old warhorse to a major facelift last year, including an all-new and stylish interior. We tested a late-1987 GT hatchback, and also drove a 1987 convertible; save for a few new paint choices, the 1988 models are no different. The Mustang's 5.0-liter V-8 was upgraded

last year with new intake and exhaust tuning, as well as revised valve timing, to produce a massive torque output of 300 lb-ft at 3200 rpm, to accompany the above-mentioned 225 bhp at 4200. This fuel injected powerhouse rumbles to life at the touch of the key and never stumbles.

Getting off the line can be touchy, however, because the clutch offers more resistance than feedback, and the window between stalling out and vaporizing the tires is more narrow than one might expect. Once underway, however, this Mustang fairly gallops as its engine spins a seamless surge of power. Sixty mph arrives in a breathless 6.2 seconds, and the quarter mile thunders past in 14.8, at 94.3 mph. The shifter is stiff and notchy but oh-so-precise, and it never misses. And the sound, oh what a sound! The sublime, snarling strains of a high-strung V-8, as rough as a burlap sack and yet as silky smooth as a lady's shoulder—at once inciting and soothing, conjuring memories of youth.

Ah yes, youth. *Road & Track* never got around to testing the GT version of the 1965 Mustang, but *Car and Driver* did (in October 1964), and the numbers its testers recorded are rather revealing. Unlaundered and unfettered, the legendary Mustang's 4.7 liters of vintage V-8 spat out 271 bhp (gross) at a peaky 6000 rpm, and an equally gross 312 lb-ft of torque at 3400—enough to wind the speedo to 60 in just 5.2 sec, and to turn the tires through the quarter mile in 14 flat, at a nice, round 100 mph.

But if this looks to you like a solid victory for free-breathing Detroit iron over Eighties electronics, you had better look again. Considering the reforms in published horsepower that have occurred since then, the 1965 machine was probably no more potent than its modern counterpart. It did weigh 393 fewer pounds, but it was also aided in its energetic sprinting by a 4.11:1 final drive. The 1987 Mustang has to climb a differential ratio of 3.08:1. C/D's number-crunchers calculated a top speed for the 1965 'Stang of just 112 mph. The 1987 model has been clocked at 148. If it were fitted with a bigger ring gear, today's Mustang would eat its legendary ancestor for lunch.

No one can deny that vehicle handling has progressed dramatically in the past 23 years; our Mustang circled the skidpad at 0.81g, a number undreamed of two decades ago. Wide

and heavy, the current Mustang lacks the razor-sharp reflexes of the best European machinery, responding with curious rubberiness to steering inputs. On-center feel is good enough, but the over-assisted steering goes numb in tight turns, and the front end floats a bit in transients. Once mastered, however, the Mustang goes where it's pointed with little enough fuss and surprising agility, slipping through our slalom at 63.6 mph. Off-throttle, its nose tends to nudge the outside of the line, but with 300 lb-ft of torque on tap, oversteer is available anytime and anywhere; you just use your right foot to choose when and how much.

The price of 0.81g is a very stiff ride, but with a proportionately stiff bodyshell, the Mustang suffers none of the violent banging, crashing and twisting that afflict the more self-consciously macho Camaro and Corvette. The Ford's live rear axle dances a bit on the bumpy stuff, but at least its cushiony seats soak up the shocks that the suspension misses.

Those very same seats are blessed with a bottom-bolster width adjustment and inflatable lumbar support, but lack meaningful bolstering for the upper half of the body. Otherwise the interior works fairly well, with simple, handsome design in the modern European fashion. The instruments themselves are large and legible, the turn-signal-stalk-cum-wiper-knob rounded and substantial. Fingertip switches activate main, fog and hazard lights plus the rear defogger. The radio and climate controls require some stretching; but the large rotary dials for the latter are exceptionally handy, while the number of tiny buttons on the former has been kept to a reasonable minimum. The two-spoke steering wheel is comfortable to hold, but a 4-spoker would be better. The driving position itself, however, nears perfection.

All of the Mustang's various virtues and vices must be considered relative to its price: just $12,106 for the GT, sans options. Even our well-equipped test car stickered for under $14,200, less than you would pay for a comparably equipped Toyota Celica GT-S. The Toyota is a fine automobile with much to recommend it, but it is no V-8-powered legend capable of nearly tripling the double nickel! How does the Mustang fare against its more obvious competitors? Well, Ford's pony can match the acceleration of the 5.7-liter Camaro IROC-Z, while offering superior passenger comfort and ergo-

nomics, as well as a more livable ride and more manageable interior sound level, against the Chevy's somewhat more precise handling. And the Ford still wins the sticker war, by more than $1000 in base price.

As we mentioned, Ford offers a convertible Mustang GT for $4500 more than the hatchback. Built by Cars and Concepts, the soft-top 'Stang suffers from considerable cowl shake but still delivers an acceptable ride. The Mustang's tall windshield effectively banishes cockpit buffeting at speeds up to 70 mph, and while its rear seat loses some width in the conversion, it still will accommodate two friendly adults, provided the top is down (head room is short with the top up). The standard-equipment power top on the car we drove had trouble reaching the windshield header, and could be latched shut only after much grunting, stretching, sweating and cursing, but previous examples were fine, so we attribute that to newness.

Certainly, whatever frustrations the convertible may present pale in comparison to the kinesthetic ecstasy of the wind in your hair and a 5.0-liter V-8 under your throttle foot. Even the hatchback GT offers a glorious trip back in time, with the windows rolled down, the stereo filling the atmosphere with rock 'n' roll, the exhaust shaking the asphalt with its thunder. It's the Mustang legend come alive, and you feel a part of it every time you take the wheel. Only the legend has never been more true, nor the Mustang ever better than it is right now.

—John F. Katz

PRICE

List price, FOB Detroit	$12,106
Price as tested	$14,158

Price as tested includes std equip.: (limited-slip diff, tilt steering wheel), custom equipment group (graphic equalizer, elect. adj mirrors, elect. window lifts, $600), special value group (central locking, AM/FM stereo/cassette, cruise control, $519), rear-window heat ($145), air cond ($788)

GENERAL

Curb weight, lb	3195
Test weight	3345
Weight distribution (with driver), f/r, %	58/42
Wheelbase, in.	100.5
Track, f/r	56.6/57.0
Length	179.6
Width	69.1
Height	52.1
Trunk space, cu ft	12.3
Fuel capacity, U.S. gal.	15.4

ENGINE

Type	ohv V-8
Bore x stroke, mm	101.6 x 76.2
Displacement, cc	4942
Compression ratio	9.0:1
Bhp @ rpm, SAE net	225 @ 4200
Torque @ rpm, lb-ft	300 @ 3200
Fuel injection	Ford multiport
Fuel requirement	unleaded, 87 pump oct

DRIVETRAIN

Transmission	5-sp manual
Gear ratios: 5th (0.68)	2.09:1
4th (1.00)	3.08:1
3rd (1.29)	3.97:1
2nd (1.93)	5.94:1
1st (3.35)	10.32:1
Final-drive ratio	3.08:1

CHASSIS & BODY

Layout	front engine/rear drive
Body/frame	unit steel
Brake system, f/r	10.8-in. vented discs/9.0-in. discs, vacuum assist
Wheels	cast alloy, 15 x 7
Tires	Goodyear Eagle VR60, 225/60VR-15
Steering type	rack & pinion, power assist
Turns, lock to lock	2.2
Turning circle, ft	41.2

Suspension, f/r: MacPherson struts, lower A-arms, coil springs, tube shocks, anti-roll bar/live axle on angled upper & lower trailing arms, coil springs, dual tube shocks, anti-roll bar

CALCULATED DATA

Lb/bhp (test weight)	14.8
Bhp/liter	45.5
Engine revs @ 60 mph in 5th gear	1800
R&T steering index	0.91

ROAD TEST RESULTS

ACCELERATION

Time to distance, sec:
0–100 ft	3.0
0–500 ft	8.2
0–1320 ft (¼ mi)	14.8
Speed at end of ¼ mi, mph	94.3

Time to speed, sec:
0–30 mph	2.1
0–40 mph	3.4
0–50 mph	4.6
0–60 mph	6.2
0–70 mph	8.7
0–80 mph	10.6
0–90 mph	13.5

SPEEDS IN GEARS

Maximum engine rpm	5900
5th gear (rpm) mph, est	(4450) 148
4th, est (5900)	136
3rd (5900)	105
2nd (5900)	75
1st (5900)	44

FUEL ECONOMY

Normal driving, mpg	16.0

BRAKES

Minimum stopping distances, ft:
From 60 mph	168
From 80 mph	289
Control in panic stop	good
Overall brake rating	fair

HANDLING

Lateral accel, 100-ft radius, g	0.81
Speed thru 700-ft slalom, mph	63.6

INTERIOR NOISE

Idle in neutral, dBA	56
Maximum, 1st gear	79
Constant 70 mph	77

ACCELERATION

Elapsed time in sec

- - - Time to distance
——— Time to speed

RAGS TO RICHES

Since the birth of the Mustang, the so-called 'pony' or 'muscle' cars have remained a key part of the American dream. They're home-grown, they're exciting — whether an IROC-Z or a Mustang GT — and they're quick. A current 5-litre Mustang GT clocks the same 14.8secs quarter-mile as the famous 5-litre 1969-70 Boss Mustang 302 homologation specials. It also has better brakes and a top speed of 148mph versus 120 for the 200lb heavier Boss 302. The 5-litre IROC-Z matches the modern Mustang's performance and is quicker on the track.

This is all fine and would be even more impressive but for the fact that the majority of pony cars bought are the plain-Jane models with base engines. These owners, however, dream of someday owning the top-of-the-line model, and these days that means a convertible. Ragtops have been pronounced dead several times in the US, the victim of safety laws and sagging consumer interest, but they keep coming back. Ford moved first with the pony cars, introducing a Mustang convertible for 1983. Chevrolet waited until the 1987 Camaros before it had an official ragtop, but dealers couldn't wait and were having convertibles made one by one at speciality shops.

Even now, neither Mustang nor Camaro convertibles come off the assembly line — they're conversions carried out by small specialist firms. Ford's are finished by Cars and Concepts, while Chevrolet depends on the American Sunroof Corporation (ASC) for its Camaros. However, both are official production models, sold through the dealer network and backed by a complete factory warranty. Farming-out speciality models is common in Detroit, where there's a mini-industry built around such conversions. ASC, for example, designed and built its own prototype Corvette for last year's Geneva Show.

To build the Camaro convertible ASC takes a partially completed T-top — the version with the lift-off glass panels which already has additional structure in the chassis, A-pillar and header.

Off comes the top and in goes the hood folding mechanism with revised metalwork between the passenger compartment and the new bootlid. The interior is redesigned to accommodate the back seats, which fold forward creating a flat luggage area — unlike the Mustang. At the rear, ASC adds a new lip spoiler that includes the US government-required high-mounted stop light.

Mustangs go through a similar process at Cars and Concepts, though the power top needs more work. The weight penalty of swapping to a soft top isn't as great as one might expect. According to Ford the Mustang saloon weighs 2751lbs; hatchback 2818lbs and convertible 2953lbs.

While the Camaro's simple top doesn't cut significantly into the rear seat area, the Mustang's more complicated system does. As a result boot space is cut by a third.

Production problems got Chevrolet off to a slow start with its Camaros in 1987, but plans call for 10,700 convertibles for 1988. Ford figures to make more than 25,000 ragtop Mustangs. Chevrolet adds $4400 (£2500) to the price of a standard Camaro,

Mustang's power *assisted top is easy to operate but it has a knuckle-busting hood cover* **The Camaro's** *hood is manual, quick to stow and produces the cleanest rear deck, but does not seal as tightly around the edge*

> ## 'Neither Mustang nor Camaro convertibles come off the production line — they're conversions carried out by specialist firms. However both carry factory warranties'

Mustang can have
*four-cylinder engine
as an option.
Standard 225bhp V8
has either four-
speed auto or five-
speed manual*
Only V8s are
*available on the
Camaro, a 5-litre
215bhp or a 225bhp
5.7-litre*

'There's no denying
the great fun of
these cars. They're
quick, the handling's
decent, and with
the top down,
they are pure joy'

and there are two versions, one just called the Convertible at about $16,250 (£9000), while the other is the famous IROC-Z version at just over $18,000 (£10,000). Only V8s are available, either a 215bhp, 5-litre with a five-speed manual or four-speed automatic, or the 225bhp 5.7-litre V8, which comes only in automatic form.

The Mustang's soft top surcharge is about $3800 (£2000), and you have the option of buying the 'luxury' LX version at around $14,000 (£8000) or the more aggressive GT model, beginning at about $17,000 (£9500). You can even get the LX convertible with a four-cylinder engine, though that seems a waste of spirit with the 225bhp 5-litre V8 available and petrol at 95 cents (54p) a gallon. After all, if the US government is going to keep the price of fuel artificially low, why not take advantage of it? Whatever the engine, a four-speed automatic or five-speed manual gearbox is available.

Despite outward similiarity, the two cars' soft tops are quite different. The Mustang has the power-assisted version — undo two levers, push a button and the top drops. By contrast, the Camaro's top is manual and quite similar to the Corvette's.

The Camaro's hood is the quickest to stow and produces the cleanest rear deck. The Mustang's is slower but completely automatic. Its drawbacks are

a tall top stack and a vinyl cover that is a knuckle-busting 3 per cent too small. You tend to leave the cover in the boot. On the other hand, its top is completely scaled around its rear edge.

In the US there are places where you can conceivably have the top down on your Mustang or Camaro on any given day of the year. When you do, you'll have to get used to people falling in love with your car. A guy in a pickup truck ogling the Camaro — a rare model in the US — almost piled into a Cadillac. A Californian cop followed it into a gas station off the freeway just to glare.

There's no denying the great fun of these cars. They're quick, the handling's decent, they make all the right noises and with the top down they are pure joy. But which to choose? There's nothing between them in acceleration, but the Ford feels the better built. Drive over a rough level crossing 1000 times and the Mustang would probably be the tightest.

In soft top terms it's a tradeoff. Midwesterners will probably take the Mustang, its better sealing paying off in their cold climate, while Californians are likely to be just as happy with the Camaro. But where the Chevvy wins decisively is in styling. The Ford is an aggressive, nicely-detailed updating — especially the GT — of a 10-year-old design. The Camaro is downright sexy.

As popular as this pair is right now, both models are at a critical point in their production lives. After months of agonising over which direction to take, Chevrolet has apparently decided to update its current pony car models for 1990 and replace them half-way through the next decade. Ford has clamped a lid on any talk of future Mustangs. It will tell you the current model will continue through to 1990 but beyond that, it is not saying. Continued production of the present model is tied to union problems in Ford's Rouge factory, which is one reason for keeping mum. But beyond that, to quote one insider: "We just don't know what's going to happen to the Mustang." ■